HOLY HOURS

Visit our web site at
www.albahouse.org
(for orders www.alba-house.com)
or call 1-800-343-2522 (ALBA)
and request current catalog

Concepción Cabrera de Armida
(Conchita)

HOLY HOURS

Translated by Sr. Dolores Icaza, rscj
and Mary McCandless

ST PAULS

Alba
House

Originally published in Spanish as *Horas Santas — Obras de Concepción Cabrera de Armida* by Editorial la Cruz, México, D.F., © by J.G. Treviño, 1962.

Library of Congress Cataloging-in-Publication Data

Conchita, 1862-1937.
  [Horas santas. English]
  Holy Hours / by Concepción Cabrera de Armida (Conchita).
    p. cm.
  ISBN 0-8189-0998-6
1. Lord's Supper—Prayer-books and devotions—English. 2. Catholic Church—Prayer-books and devotions—English. I. Title.

  BX2215.C63 2006
  242—dc22

                2005024662

Produced and designed in the United States of America by the Fathers and Brothers of the Society of St. Paul,
2187 Victory Boulevard, Staten Island, New York 10314-6603, as part of their communications apostolate.

ISBN: 0-8189-0998-6

Printing Information:

Current Printing - first digit   1 2 3 4 5 6 7 8 9 10

Year of Current Printing - first year shown

2006   2007   2008   2009   2010   2011   2012   2013   2014

Contents

Preface

When you listen to a beautiful love song, do you examine each word? And if some lyrics manifest a pathos or a joy that goes beyond your own, do you turn down the volume, not to hear the melody? I doubt it.

For those of us nowhere near the height or depth of Venerable Conchita's union with Jesus, there may be a moment when listening to her love song that we want to close the book because the pathos and joy of it is higher and deeper than our own level. Yet we find that we can't drop it. Why?

When reading *Holy Hours*, I seemed to hear my Jesus tell me not to give up because my prayer is so inferior to Conchita's, but rather to sing her song for now, only in a "lower key." For example, when Conchita asks Jesus for more and more sufferings, I could just ask for the grace not to make such a fuss over the sufferings that come along unbidden.

Meditative reading of *Holy Hours* speaks to a place in our hearts we don't always want to go. Why? Perhaps because there is a part of us that does not want to be too intimate with Jesus. "Love is not loved," Saint Mary Magdalene de Pazzi used to proclaim. Once those words rang in my soul and I asked Jesus why I was so shy about loving Him as Love.

— *Is it easier for me to love You as truth because truth is strong and love is vulnerable?*

— *Is it easier for me to love You as beauty because beauty is sublime and love is messy?*

— *Is it easier for me to love You as mercy because mercy is balm and love is strenuous?*

I told Jesus that as I looked into His tragic eyes, I wondered if the reason I was afraid of love might be deeper still.

Have I a terror of surrender to Your divine Heart whose beat is so loud I could no longer hear my own?

Or, still more simply, that I could refuse You nothing, no matter how painful, if I was close enough to know You wanted it!

I heard Jesus telling me that I could not experience the fullness of His love for me if I was afraid to come closer. "Perfect love casts out fear." Surrender!

Conchita's spirituality is precisely a proof of the depth we all could go in experiencing the love of Jesus were we to surrender totally.

Don't we want, just as Conchita did, "to kiss those pale and mute lips, which spoke only tenderness and breathed only charity"? (Holy Hour 3)

Don't we want, just as Conchita did, "to try to think inside of Jesus — not just live, but think with His very thoughts, so saintly, so immaculate, and as transparent as the sky without clouds... just and non-judgmental"? (Holy Hour 7)

Don't we want, just as Conchita did, "to perform our works in a supernatural manner... (rather than) routinely, thus, lazily, without stirring up fervor, scattered and without spirit"? (Holy Hour 13)

Don't we want, just as Conchita did, "to make our lives a tapestry of acts of love that may serve as both wrapping and life for all our virtues"? (Holy Hour 14)

Don't we want, just as Conchita did, "to

hide in the depth of the rock, to be cured and become happy"? (Holy Hour 17)

Don't we want, just as Conchita did, "to cheer up, and be brave"? (Holy Hour 21)

Yes, yes, yes, yes, yes!

Now, as you begin to join the heart of Venerable Conchita in her Holy Hour prayers, ask the Holy Spirit to make you at least long to long for the transforming union that was hers.

Ronda Chervin, Ph.D.

(Ronda Chervin, Ph.D., is a professor of philosophy and religious studies and the author of many books about Catholic spirituality, including *The Kiss from the Cross* and *Becoming a Handmaid of the Lord*.)

HOLY HOURS

For every day of the month,
dedicated to persons devoted to the
Sacred Heart of Jesus

Preparatory prayers for each day

— Let us place ourselves consciously before the presence of God.

— I adore You, my Lord, with all the affection I am capable of; I humbly outstretch my hands toward You, asking for a ray of Your light for my intelligence, and for a spark of Your fire to purify my heart, so that everything in me, lost in You, may give You glory during this meditation, and that Your grace may come upon my lowly soul. Amen.

Editor's note:

Each Holy Hour is meant to be read as a step-by-step meditation. In this text, an ellipsis (…) indicates an opportunity to pause for meditative reflection.

1

HOLY HOUR

To Descend

Spiritual Setting: To contemplate Jesus at the Praetorium of Pilate, who points Him out and says, "Behold the man..." *because He almost no longer was* — being *Who He is* — because of the extent of His humiliation. He was a worm... not a man... an outcast, rejected, the shame of all men.

Petition: With all the strength of our souls, let us ask to be humbled before everybody, so as to be like Jesus.

Practice: During this week, our first thought will be: *"How can we become more humble...* strive to win the last post, the last place, the most humble tasks and *everything that affronts our pride and arrogance?"*

Why did Jesus descend? Only because He loved me. There was no motive other than the greatness, the immensity of His love, that made Him descend even to the point of folly.

But just as He always acts for loving purposes which I often do not understand, in His descent to nothingness and ultimate humiliation, He had the purpose of teaching me the way to happiness and how to conquer heaven.

The Lord descended so I could learn to be meek and humble of heart.

"O My child! 'Why did I *descend*?' you ask Me. Only to make you happy... only so you would be loving and desirous of the humility which is so costly to your nature.

"Hesitate no longer to follow in My footsteps... forget yourself... stop worrying about yourself... think about Me often and you will see how easy self-denial is, how easy the perfect surrender of your will. What else is humility but perfect participation in My Eucharistic life, in My human life, that is — and was — continual humility?

"Humility is the life of love and this is how love is proved — this is how I loved you, lowering Myself, annihilating Myself, disappearing, so as to infuse in you, later, soul of the Cross, this *need*, this *color*, this unforgettable resemblance to the Beloved of your soul. This is the reason I came down: to attract you with Calvary's perfume of self-denial, of disgrace, of mockery and scorn... to a most perfect union with Me: you must breathe humility and the Cross.... This is *why* I came down, but *how* did I descend?"

"I came down in an unimaginable descent, to make Myself man, but... O child of My soul, I still descended even further, taking responsibility for the sins of the world. And sin, what ransom does it require? Well, this is what I wished to lay upon Myself — the justice of My Father — and for this I annihilated Myself... I descended... I humiliated Myself, child, and made Myself as nothing for your love.

"And for this reason, I was born in an animal stable! Although I was the Splendor of the Father, I descended to the world in a stable... and if the angels had not revealed this to the shepherds, only the beasts would have been there to keep Me company!

"And I *descended* to the circumcision, publicly accepting this mark of sin.

"And I was presented in the Temple like any other sinner, *descending*.

"And I *descended*, fleeing from a man, to Egypt, making My powerlessness evident.

"And I *descended* from the Temple to Nazareth to hide My zeal, My wisdom and My radiance.

"And I *descended*, choosing work that would always keep Me in a humble place, that of a carpenter.

"I *descended* — living unknown and forgotten, poor and scorned.

"'Can anything good come out of Nazareth?' the people said, yet from there I chose to come forth, always choosing that which was scorned and despicable. I made Myself as nothing because I chose it, and I chose it because I loved you!

"*Descending* was always My consolation, My beloved child, My meditation, My illusion, My LIFE!

"At My baptism, when John refused to baptize Me — out of respect, out of love, because he knew Who I was — I insisted, saying to him, '*It is fitting* that I humble Myself to the point of nothingness.'

"In the desert I lived all alone among the animals, descending, always descending, because lowering Myself in this life was My strongest passion.

"I humbled Myself, and how much so being God, and allowing Satan to tempt Me, to carry Me along as a toy to the pinnacle of the Temple!

"And when the multitudes, attracted by My charm, and My doctrine, desired to exalt Me,

I hid Myself, miraculously disappearing. But this was only because I wanted to descend, never ascend, *except to Calvary*, because this would be My extreme humiliation.

"I lowered Myself referring all glory to My Father.

"If they asked Me for miracles, I prayed to My Father before accomplishing them, and I attributed them to My Father. I was nobody; that is, *I considered Myself as nothing*, so as to cure you from your pride.

"Whenever they praised My goodness, I answered, 'Only God is Holy.' Even though I did not have a human person, and *My Ego* was divine, My humanity nevertheless *was humbled*.

"In spite of the Divinity that I carried within Me, I lived shamed and martyred... carrying sin upon Myself made Me blush, and thus I abased Myself.

"And when Peter, My Apostle, wanted to prevent My abasement and My suffering, I rejected him as Satan: 'Go away, do you want Me not to drink of My Father's cup?'

"And at the Apostles' feet, and even at Judas' feet, *I lowered Myself.*

"And in the institution of the Eucharist and in every Communion, I descend, I lower Myself, I abase Myself even to the incredible, descending to make Myself the most common and trivial food — *bread*, and annihilating Myself even more when entering into impure hearts.

"And on that night, such a *cruel* night, My child, I descended to being the dregs of the populace.

"And the Wisdom of the Father was taken for a fool; your Jesus for a fool, and thus did all the nations see Me on that Good Friday, descending, O My child, drowning Myself in humiliation, mockery, and sarcasm.

"And I was scourged… and proclaimed as false king… and traded for Barabbas and I almost *was no more*, so they presented Me saying: 'Behold the man,' because I was barely recognizable, to such an extreme had I descended.

"And I rolled, falling three times to the level of the earth among the feet of My executioners, lowering Myself, choosing a scaffold of criminals for My death.

"I was crucified between two thieves so as *to descend,* so as to mistakenly be taken as one of them and thus die full of shame, as the king of humiliation and abasement. Because of My love for you, child of My Heart, I became the dregs of the populace, the scum of the earth, a worm and not a man!

"This is the reason that to cite My name is to cite humility. And this is what I expect of you: that as a devoted soul you may be also recognized for your humility, signaling the same.

"What is it you are going to tell Me? How are you going to humble yourself?"

Jesus of all my soul, I will lower myself with *eagerness*, with *madness*, with *constancy*, and with *love,* without ever reaching the bottom.

I will descend by beginning all the works of the day with an act of profound humility, considering my nothingness and my unworthiness.

I will descend considering that everything that is not hell is a favor for me.

If You give me solace, I will not rest; rather, with great thankfulness, I will return Your gifts and remain joyfully in my own poverty.

When I fail, I will humble myself without losing my peace, confiding more fully in You and distrusting myself all the more... because if Satan beats me in arrogance, I overtake him in my stubbornness and in my recidivism in sin.

I will humble myself by discovering my faults, the rottenness of my soul and of all my wounds *without detour, without disguise.*

I will descend, never diminishing my guilt, and even when I am not guilty, I will keep silence, and appear guilty.

I will lower myself in my own house considering myself a beggar to whom food is given in charity and compassion. I will never be demanding and always be grateful for anything they do for me.

I will rejoice when others are praised and

exalted, while I will only have a saintly pride in my great misfortunes, another reason to awaken Your compassion for me, my Jesus.

If they praise me, I will humble myself, bringing my deficiencies, imperfections and so many defects to balance it out, and at least mentally, always wholeheartedly putting myself at the feet of others.

I will ask Jesus for everything that may honor my neighbors and have them loved and exalted: and for myself — O, yes, contempt, scorn, helplessness, disdain, nullity!

I will never judge the actions of my superiors or my brethren, loving them with humility, not stopping to see the defects they might have. I will offer myself to do the most humble works, for these will be as perfume to You, my Jesus, and will more greatly bear the scent of Calvary.

Since I have contemplated Your humiliations, my Lord, this has been my ideal: to always and constantly descend, to never rise again. This is what I want, my Beloved, for this my heart thirsts.

What else did You do, *Life of my life, but descend*, demanding with all the tones of Your Heart, *obscurity*, *helplessness*, *annihilation*, and *smallness*?

These exaggerations absorbed You. You, Love of my life! And all of Your tendencies were to look for greater and greater depths and abysses toward which You could descend. Nothing was enough to satisfy the ardors that inflamed Your divine Heart to descend further. And what else could I do other than to unite myself to You and disappear?

Yes, Jesus, most humble Jesus. I promise this to You before the Sacrament of Your love.

Admiration and tenderness overcome me, and when I contemplate You — not I, but the Lord's grace within me, as Saint Paul said, will make me imitate You in the bottomless abyss of Your voluntary obscurity.

I desire to live of Your own life and heartbeats, and sink so You may reign, and become *nothing* so You, my Jesus, may be everything!

Each day I wish not only to descend, but to *be less* — in my body by means of penance, and in my soul by withdrawing from self, diminishing the old self… annihilating my ego… leaving my own free will… cutting off and pruning my miseries, and filling up the perfect vacuum of myself, so that I may truly say: *not I, but Jesus in me.*

O my most humble Virgin, you who imitated Jesus in all your being! Give me that virtue by which the Lord chose you to be His mother. Amen.

2

HOLY HOUR

Do Not Fear

Spiritual Setting: Today we will contemplate Jesus, Who with a most amiable face… so soothing and full of peace, says to us, *"Do not fear, I am your Jesus,"* and with this, everything is already said.

Petition: Let us ask the Lord, with all the ardor of our hearts, the grace to respond to so much kindness and to such love by being generous toward Him.

Practice: A purity of heart even more than angelic so that Jesus may be able to trust us, and thus we may really console Him.

"Do not fear, My child; come to Me with confidence, *because confidence is the last word of love —* and a confident love born of purity of heart *is what should form here on earth the perfumed environment for Jesus to breathe.*

"Do not fear... if up until now you have been unfaithful... ungrateful... a sinner and less gentle with Me. See, I am the Lamb of God Who takes away the sins of the world.... It is for this that My Precious Blood is daily at your disposal, so you can drink it... so you may purify yourself... so you may become holy receiving My Divinity, its substance which is purity itself. Do not fear!

"If you have Me, your Jesus, what can you fear?

"My Heart has sighed for you; My eyes have cried for you. My feet have been tired because of you. My Blood has poured over you, bathing you; My very flesh has fed you for so many years, communicating to you My own substance. What can you fear? Am I not your father, your mother, and your brethren, your friend, your spouse and your Beloved, chosen from among thousands? So then, child, what is there that can make you fear?

"Do not fear — because it is I Who is talking to you from this immaculate Host. If you waver, why do you fear — is it not I who am your fortress? If you are in the darkness, why do you fear, if I am your light? If you feel cold, why do you fear, if I am your heat? If you are weak, why do you fear, My child, if I am your food, and if My memory alone can invigorate you? If I put you to the test, O little child of My soul, do you not understand that it is to multiply your merits, to strengthen you in virtue, so you can be Mine even more, to shape My Cross in you? If I am already your recompense… if I shall always be your recompense, what can you fear? Speak, speak, I want to listen to your voice… to wipe your tears and let you know *Who I am*."

Second Meditation

"I have listened to you, My child, but I still repeat to you, and I will repeat it a thousand times: *'Do not fear, for I am here.'* I live with you…. I do not lose you from My sight for a minute… and understand that I am the God of *peace*… the *patient* God… the enamored God… a God Who does not fear to infinitely abase Himself, O My child! The God Who *begs to be loved*. My love for you is so great *that I have become a beggar for love*… and it is because you have cost Me so much… and also because you are going to give Me much *glory*. This is why I desire to infuse confidence in you… because My plan is to make My chosen souls fall in love with everything that the world abhors and despises… with that which worldly human nature dreads… with everything that the Word loved, annihilating Himself for love's sake!

"And could you fear any and all enemies, being in My arms, as My arms are the Cross? O My beloved child! *I have been with you for such a long time and you still do not know Me!* Do you not know My goodness? Have you still not studied your Jesus?

"In Bethlehem I gave peace. In Nazareth, I did not know anything other than to obey. During My public life, I was always gentle. To the half-broken reed I said, 'Do not fear; I will not break you.' To the smoldering wick, I said, 'Do not fear, I will not extinguish you.' To the poor, I said, 'Do not fear, I will be your treasure.' To those who cried, I said, 'Do not fear, I shall be your consolation.' To the blind man, I said, 'Do not fear, I will restore the light.' To the lost sheep, I said, 'Do not fear, I am the Good Shepherd.' To the prodigal son, I said, 'Do not fear, I am your Father.' During My sorrowful Passion, I remained meek and humble, silent and full of love, presenting My Body to martyrdom, encountering suffering.

"Here in the Eucharist more than in any other place, My Heart has cried out for twenty centuries, 'Do not fear, it is I, despite the humble cloth that covers Me. I am He, Who with the most tender expression of love, asks you to have confidence, purity, and sacrifice, as well as an expanded holiness. I only ask for My Cross as a bed… some loving arms… a lily-like heart where I can rest. Do you still fear, beloved of Jesus?"

THIRD MEDITATION

No, my Jesus, love of my soul, I will no longer fear… enraptured by joy, I listen to You and contemplate You, entranced, greatly enjoying that You are the only God of my love and of my expectations. And in thankfulness for Your graciousness, and in proportion to my great misery, You are going to receive today, my Sweet Lord of the Eucharist, proof of my great love.

You say to me, my Jesus, "Do not fear, it is I," and I, a vile earthworm, desire to say the same thing to You, "Do not fear, Lord, it is I."

Jesus of my soul, from now on I will no longer be that soul who has offended You so much through sin, tepidity, and infidelity, self-love, concealment, disobedience, impatience and ingratitude. No, my Jesus, do not fear for this soul any longer, this soul who expects everything from Your grace, and who from now on will be crucified and will *deny itself* for Your sake.

Do not fear, my Love, that my promises

will deceive You, that my promises should be vain, that my kisses would betray You. It is a loving soul who is speaking to You; do not fear, my Dear, do not fear anything from Your poor child, who dies to serve You, to adore You, to respond to Your love.

Saint Peter sinned, but cried, and *Jesus was not wary of him, because He knew that Peter loved Him.* Judas kissed Him: but *Jesus was wary of him, because Judas did not love Him.* It has been said, "The wounds from someone who loves you are less fearful than the treacherous kisses of the one who loves you not."

Let us then love Jesus, crying and proving our love for Him *with works* because in this way our kisses will be saintly and will console Him.

Let nothing of the world tarnish our soul… for nothing upon earth may compromise us in relation to self-denial. Let us disappear completely from our own sight, not having any other life, any other desires, any other will than that of Jesus. He never believes to have descended enough, and I, despicable mud, will I let myself be won over by humility? It never seemed to Him that He had extended His arms sufficiently *to receive the Cross,* and will I, in closing my arms, let myself be won over by generosity? No, no, I shall run in the way of perfection so Jesus will not fear me. Let Him fear sinners, those who do not love Him, those who deceive Him, but I shall not be thus, and after the next Holy Hour I will approach the Altar, and say humbly but confidently — O, yes, I will say, my beloved Eucharistic Jesus, I will say to You a thousand times, "Do not fear, my Love, it is I who love You, who adore You, who dies to console You, to be Your comfort, to dry Your tears, to be a host in union with You."

RESPONSE

Is it not true, my Jesus, that whenever You hear a voice near to You that says to You, *"It is I,"* You will not fear? How could You fear in Your resting place? How would You not sleep quietly, Lord, confiding in the devotees of Your Cross? If in some occasion, my Love, You have been afraid in this blessed little place… if unfortunately sometimes You have trembled in Your Tabernacle for mistrust of the souls that approached it, O, my Jesus, I can hardly believe it! Now it will no longer be so, and You shall be comforted, my dear Jesus, among canticles of love, and happily and quietly You will rest among the perfumes of most pure lilies, and You will rest Your glances without fear upon the souls transformed into a Cross, only to please You.

My beloved Virgin, give me an unlimited confidence for Jesus' Heart, so full of tenderness. Amen.

3

HOLY HOUR

To Paint Jesus in Our Heart

Spiritual Setting: Contemplate Jesus crucified, nailed to the Cross for our sins; with all the tenderness of our souls let us fix His image in our minds so that we might imitate it.

Petition: Today, with ardent and fervent souls we shall ask that the Lord Himself may trace His outline on our bodies and in our souls with the paintbrush of the Cross so that we can resemble Him.

Practice: During this week we shall allow the divine Artist to realize His divine pleasure in our souls for love alone.

Jesus of my soul, just see how You are, all red and bathed in Your own blood so that I may be able to drink from it, to quench my thirst for the Eucharist.... O, if only I could squeeze my veins and return to You love for love... blood for blood... sacrifice for sacrifice!

You die to give me life. O, my Beloved, do not look at me with those eyes broken by Your agony.... I want to see them happy, joyous with the brightness of the purity and glory with which they always shine.

It breaks my heart to see You shattered so... but *this is my own doing*. Nevertheless, from this moment on I wish to soothe and comfort You with the purity of my heart, my breath, and my tenderness, giving You only caresses and all the fire of my heart, my vitality, my very being, hiding You inside the depths of my spirit.

Ah, my Jesus Victim, I want to imitate You to the depths of my soul, transforming myself into another crucified by love! Ah, how I wish to make myself like You so as to be a true child of Mary.

My heart is going to be the canvas... the colors, the virtues; the palette, humility — and those virtues — do You wish them to be mortification, penance, scorn, self-denial, submission of judgment, silence and obedience? O, yes, because Your child wants all of this, and much more, wrapping all of these acts with love.

Isn't it right that the devotee of the Crucified should be crucified?

Come again my Beloved; come my adorable Jesus for I never tire of contemplating You.

SECOND MEDITATION

O, my Life! With tenderness, I am going to heal that most pure forehead riddled with so many wounds!

With all my love I am going to untangle that hair soaked in Blood.

I am going to caress Your black and blue cheeks with my loving kisses.

I will also kiss those pale and mute lips, which spoke only tenderness and breathed only charity, thousands and thousands of times, for they are also mine.

Let us cast away that crown — the thorns are only for me; for You, the stars, the brightest stars — not pain. Is this what You want, my Love?

And that red breast… and that volcano of charity, and that wound, and that fire?… Jesus, what can I say if Your Heart burns me?

And why those holes in Your hands and in Your feet? O, my Jesus, if they would crucify You again, they would have to pierce my heart with the nails before I would allow them to reach Your holy flesh.

And those bruised knees, Your back broken into pieces... and Your most holy, virginal body — dislocated.

And those ears that heard only blasphemies before being closed.

That Incarnate Word made flesh so cruelly shattered.

What can I do for You, my Love?

Just see how my tears soak your head, your face, your whole body. And why not, if You are all mine?

Ah, my Lord! Your poor child dies for love of You, and claims You, and calls You her own and envelops You with blood because this child has no wings to cover You. With tears I wipe away, or want to wipe away, the ingratitude of a world that does not care if it crucifies You. But how can I console You? Not with tears and desires, but with deeds, tracing Your divine image in my body and in my soul.

THIRD MEDITATION

O, my Jesus, my eyes will not see except through Your own eyes and with their same tenderness and charity.

My ears will no longer hear except through Your ears, suffering and forgetting.

I will speak through Your lips, my Jesus, and my heart will be Your own Heart…, and its beating my own heartbeats, and Your Will be my will… and Your pleasure, my pleasure.

But You, my Love, had nothing but the Cross and thorns in every manner and everywhere.… You heard nothing but slander and ingratitude; You tasted nothing but gall and vinegar…, and scourging, fatigue, hunger, and thirst were Your inheritance and Your life.… All wounds, all pain. When You died, Your robe was blood… for You to rest on, only rough wood… for a pillow, a bouquet of thorns.… Without a piece of earth, He Who created the whole universe.… Without a drop of water, He Who created the seas.… Without father, without mother; Your only property, just three nails that made You suffer terribly, supporting You; for comfort, desertion; for company, the Cross.… O, Jesus, my Jesus, what does my heart feel?

But You, my Jesus, in the midst of all these sufferings, *You loved… You burned…* Your divine Heart was set on fire, consumed by millions of degrees of heat, for souls; Lord, grant that even though my heart may shatter into pieces a thousand times, it may also be embraced and consumed for the same cause! O, yes! my mission is to acquire graces, but "every grace comes from Calvary and has the character and hue of its origin." This is why I desire to suffer, Jesus of my soul: with the brush of the Cross, I wish to paint You in my soul with the most vivid colors of love and sacrifice. You shall suffer no longer because Your children are here to complete Your Passion; Jesus, Jesus of the soul, may we be the balm that heals Your wounds and the comfort that quickens Your love.

From now on, my exterior will be Jesus… and my interior will also be Jesus… a Jesus tender and meek of Heart, with His modesty, purity, obedience, and poverty, with the same tendency toward suffering and self-denial, with the same blood, soul, and life.

Love receives consolation when it suffers, and this is the consolation we ask of You today, Beloved of our souls: a love that is not satisfied until You transform us into the living image we so ardently love.

Response

O Jesus of all my soul, most beloved Jesus. My heart aches; it is torn to pieces by an ardent desire to reflect You in it, to absorb You, to duplicate You in its depth. Suffering gives it a new ardor, and it thinks only about resembling You.

My Jesus, I desire to sacrifice myself for Your sake, to give myself up to You, but abundantly, without those petty calculations of souls who do not love You. O, who could die for You! If only I could squeeze all the blood from my veins for You, all the blood of my heart! I would like to give You all the sap of my life, to wring myself as grapes in the press, giving You everything that I am, drop by drop. O, yes! I would even like to see myself thus: like fired clay, like a dry leaf, like dust that everyone could trample on.

Ah, Jesus! I die for You through love, and would like to be a Seraph of love and a martyr in suffering! At least grant that I may love You above all the suffering and all the joy of creatures and things... more than Your gifts and even more than heaven itself. Grant me that love, superior to everything that is not You, and which is capable of lifting me above the earth, and make me live a completely supernatural and divine life. Only through that immense love can I be transformed into Your own image. But no, there exists something else that will transform me into You more rapidly, and this is the Eucharist — that Eucharist which is my life, my breath, my treasure, my being. Ah, Lord, it has been said that the ermine feeds itself with snow and that is why it is white — I desire *to feed myself on the Eucharist* to be able to become a victim. Thus and only in this way shall I live on Your substance: I will savor Your Blood; Your suffering will be my suffering, and Your love shall be my love.

Mary, celestial Virgin! Paint your most beloved Jesus on all of my being! Amen.

4

HOLY HOUR

How He Loves Me

Spiritual Setting: See Jesus bending over my ear, taking my tired head between His divine hands, and setting it with fatherly tenderness upon His shoulder, saying these things to me.

Petition: I will ask today for a willing ear to listen to the Beloved, and not to let the slightest word from His sacred lips escape me.

Response: An unlimited gratitude, seclusion, and receptiveness of heart in order to meditate upon His delightful words, ashamed of my own coldness.

"It is in *humbling oneself*, My child," says His melodious and gentle voice, like a dove's cooing, like a penetrating breeze, like a soft, enchanting whisper that passes by. "I *loved you...* annihilating Myself... and atoning.

"I loved you and gave Myself up for you... and I became man... and made Myself a slave..., became bread, became a worm!

"I loved you, dear child, and I delighted in spilling My very last drop of Blood to buy heaven for you.

"I loved you as nobody has ever loved you, from eternity to eternity... with an infinite love, with the love of a God! I never loved Myself without also loving you.

"I loved you with the great love of a friend... of a brother... of a mother... of a *Jesus...* and I love you moreover and above all, with a *humble love...* from Heart to heart.

"I love you because it pleases me to come down to you... annihilating Myself... to atone for sin.

"I loved you in order to raise you from the hopelessness in which you found yourself, and because of this I did not mind descending, even though I am God, annihilating Myself until I could no more.

"I loved you with a love as grand as My

mercy. Can you understand this, or at least be grateful for this love?

"What have you done up until now with this torrent of tenderness with which My goodness has covered you? Forgotten it, child of My Heart… trampled upon it, despised it, and preferred earth to heaven?"

Second Meditation

O my Love, Jesus of my soul, fire of my life! Why is it that I do not know how to consume myself in sacrifice — purifying myself to thank You for Your kindness? I will love You more and more every day, with a love always growing in purity, in ardor, and in crucifixion. With Saint Augustine, I will say, "Why is it that I do not have an infinite love so as to love an infinite love?" I shall be a victim of Your glory, of Your will, leaving my own will and crucifying myself in Your honor.

Jesus does not have pity for Himself, because He has pity on me, such a miserable one! And that is why He sought cruelty, torture, mockery, and the most infamous scorn for Himself; and for me, who earned hell: caresses… the tenderness of a God-man, three times saintly and a thousand times a mother.

He loves me even to the point of being my

daily food in Holy Communion, communicating His own more-than-angelic substance to me, more than the Seraphim and the Cherubim, His purity… His humility… His obedience… His self-denial… His charm… His delight and all His virtues.

He Who is Heaven, communicates heaven, and He Who is suffering, communicates the Cross to attract the Father's most holy gaze toward us, and to inflame us with the divine fire of the Holy Spirit, consuming all of our misery.

And not only does He feed my soul with His lily-white Body and with His Blood that begets virgins, but even more with *His memory*… which is another type of nourishment that gives life, sanctifies, and sets on fire.

That powerful attraction with which He wins souls, those close brushes with His divinity… that absorption, that possession, that deification in Him, what else can it be but love?

Those kisses of the soul, that divine soaking, that strengthening of union that gives the life of the spirit itself, giving Him acts of love, being, air, heat, and existence — what can it be but the way He loves us?

When one feels His divine forehead, His profile, His features, His charm and beauty, the soul is left abstracted… absorbed… speechless… and full of light, of purity, of solitude — what can this be called, my Jesus, but love?

And when even the memory of this is enough for the soul to remain transfixed by a subtle suffering, and this suffering brings forth remembrance; and that remembrance pain, feeling as though Jesus is tracing Himself on the soul. O! Is this not a very deep and great love?

These are the marvels of God's love in souls! Let us adore Him and with our humility and purity try to be worthy to receive them.

Third Meditation

And if Jesus loves me as His Father loved Him — is it not right, lovable, and desirable that I crucify myself in whatever form, and with a martyrdom of love?

O, yes, Jesus of my soul! Grant me the joy, the priceless grace of suffering much for You! … Because children of Your Heart were born to suffer and endure, what do they do when they do not accomplish this? … I thirst to ask You, to stretch out my hand, to beg for pain, more pain to compensate for Your love, in my limitation.… My heart expands, Lord; my soul delights before this horizon so that I am anxious to extend with new energies, with a celestial start, when I contemplate Your love!

And if Jesus loves me as He loves His Father then this means He loves me in His same

Being, replicating Himself in me through an ardent desire for humility, zeal, purity and self-denial, obedience and poverty. And would I be able to say without blushing that He finds the joy that He is looking for in me, and forms His love, loving me?

He loves in the Father and in the Holy Spirit. Do I find myself between those Divine Persons with a life that is all pure… absorbed… interior… with unawareness of self, solitude, and a lack of worldliness… in a most loving union?

He loves me, looking for the fabric of my heart to live in the midst of it, and so it does not amaze me that He makes me *see Him dwell* in my heart in the fabric of that consecrated Host that I contemplate before my eyes.

He loves me, asking me, a beggar, what I can give to others: my love, my kisses, my tenderness, my affection and my suffering, and finally, my body, my heart, my life, my nights and my days; my thoughts and my senses and faculties; my time and my eternity. O, my God, my God! And is this not love?

This is charity… this is mercy… this is the humiliation of a God made man.… *This is how Jesus loves me!*

Response

O, Jesus of all my soul! What can I give You,
what can I say to You overwhelmed by the huge
weight of Your holy love? Today I will give You
my heart, my life, my liberty, those kisses of the
soul that spring up from the very bosom of grateful love, kisses that contain oceans of respectful
tenderness, born of my love for You. Alienated,
I want to kiss Your feet, Love of my life, Your
hands, Your very Heart, even if I should be
pricked by the thorns, so much the better, because I desire to be fastened to it forever.

Jesus, let me love You without limit… caress You and cry amid tears, so as to console You
without reserving anything for myself in my immolation as a victim.

If love crucified You for my sake, let that
same love, O, Jesus, crucify me for You!

Mary, sweetness and charm of all hearts: I
desire to love your Jesus as He loved me. Amen.

5

HOLY HOUR

How I Love Him

Spiritual Setting: Today I will see Jesus come near to me, asking very sweetly: "And you, child, how do you love Me?"

Petition: I will ask the Lord to purify my heart and my lips before I talk to Him to tell Him truly what my heart feels for Him.

Response: All day long, to feel the words I have spoken enthusiastically reassuring Jesus of how I love Him, and of how much I love Him.

O, Jesus, my Eucharistic Jesus! You ask me how I love You: "Do you love Me more than these?" You say this to me with both Your lips and Your Heart…. "How do you love Me, My child?" Your enchanting voice repeats it to me, because, O yes, because You long to know it and my lips tell You in every tone!

What can I say, Lord, Lord? … a little or a lot? … with words or with actions? … with sensitivity or with harshness? … with purity or with the darkness of ingratitude? See, Jesus, how my heart trembles… see how my tears dim my eyes… see how my strength fails and my breast feels oppressed… and sobs suffocate me… and my voice extinguishes itself without knowing how to respond to You, Heaven of my life.

Why do You ask me about what You are seeing? What can I answer You, Soul of my soul? Forgetting my own unworthiness, allow me to let the ardent lava of my breast's volcano flow and break the dike of loving respect, shouting in Your ear a thousand times:

I love You, yes, I love You; I love You so much and I love You a million times, in every heartbeat… in every breath, in every moment!

I love You with a thousand martyrdoms of love!

I love You with the very intimate and indescribable subtleties of tenderness!

I love You as a father, as a mother, as a friend and as a spouse; more so than all mothers love their children... with Your same love, because I receive You in my heart every day.

I love You with madness, with delirium, as the realized ideal of my soul, which goes beyond what eye has seen, or what the mind can understand, as Saint Paul used to say. Who can recount, O Jesus, Your delights, Your charm, Your enchantment? Who can explain that Divinity which hides itself in that consecrated Host, that draws us, fascinates us, attracts us and moves us?

Jesus, You are the ideal of purity... of self-denial... of abasement... of poverty... of those thousands and thousands of heroic and perfect virtues that I pursue and desire, with You, to make my own.

You, Eucharist of my life, are everything for me... and I could not live without that daily food that, consuming me, gives me life... and that increases my strength so as *to love more, to suffer more.*

You open Your arms every morning and I embrace You with the entire effusiveness of my tenderness.

You open Your Heart to me and I throw myself into it to burn... to caress You, I call even before dawn comes and full of thirsty and ardent love I wait for You.... As the moth turns to the light, my soul, with all its tendencies throws itself into the fire of Your Heart, Jesus, losing itself in You.... "Come in," You say to me, "Come in," I tell You.... And in our finding each other, Your fire penetrates me... Your light illuminates me... Your Blood comforts me... Your Heart burns me... Your charms delight me... and Your suffering inebriates me. O, Jesus, Jesus, Jesus! Is it not true that this is how I love You?

SECOND MEDITATION

Your eyes tell me that You are still not satisfied and that You want me to continue, and I am going to proceed, my Lord!

Ah, Jesus, my Jesus!

I love You as a little Child and at Calvary... in Your exile and in Your preaching... at Nazareth and at the Cenacle... at the Garden and at Tabor... blessing the children and tied up as a criminal.

I love You scourged and treated as a fool... at the Praetorium and at the Jordan... and at the well of Samaria, in the Temple and on the Cross.

At every site, Jesus, Jesus, Your charms enamor me, Your delights attract me, and Your goodness overwhelms me.

I love You in the Sepulcher and in the

Resurrection… in the Ascension and in the Eucharist.

I love You, my Dear, transfigured and soaked in blood; with thorns and with light, with nails and glorified.

Every action of Your holy life… every word pronounced by Your divine lips… every beat of Your human Heart moves me… teaches me… dumbfounds me… and Your holy love drives me mad.

Your gazes draw me… Your smiles make me surrender… Your humility annihilates me… Your sweetness embarrasses me… Your self-denial makes me blush… and Your pain and suffering trace themselves in the depths of my soul, bewildering me.

And all of Your love and suffering cries out to me very loudly, "LOVE! SUFFER!" and I want to love unto delirium… and I want to suffer unto martyrdom.

And, Jesus, I feel the echo of Your whole life in my being, reverberating upon me and pushing me to be *pure*… to be *loving*… and to be a *victim*.

If You have loved me crucifying Yourself for me, from now on I will crucify myself for the good and for the guilty, for the just, and for the sinners.

And my tenderness and my kisses, and my body and my soul, and my nights and my days, and my time and my heart, and my love and my suffering are for You and shall be only for You.

And I take You with me everywhere I go in the depth of my soul as the King of my thoughts and of my will.

And Lord, I give You everything I have and everything I do not have.

And my memory of You is my life, and my pleasure and my pain do not exist without Your being their owner, and without Your participating in them.

And it grieves me to not love You, Jesus, and I am delirious over possessing You… and I dream about You at night and I delight in You during the day… and I eat You, and I drink You… and I inhale You and I exhale You… and very often I remain spellbound by Your charms … by Your beauty… by Your charity… by Your tenderness!

And the nearness to You in Communion purifies me…. Your contact with my lowly heart sanctifies me… and my soul is always speaking about You, speaking with You… and the thought of You vivifies my soul… and fortifies it and Your company makes it joyful!

And my heart burns inside of Yours… and the fire of both hearts fuses them… and the sufferings are only one suffering… and the loves are only one love.

Are You satisfied, my Jesus?

Jesus, Jesus of all my heart! Can You tell me this is not true, Lord of my soul? Can You tell me this is not the way in which Your poor child loves You... that it is not just a single sigh which gives us life... that it is not just a single fire that devours us...? Tell me, if You can, my Beloved, that the glory of Your Father, the salvation of the world and the perfection of souls are not the goal of this heart, its passion and the only dream of its existence!

Tell me if You can, that the sound of Your soul does not resound in my own lowly soul which says, "*Cross, purity; purity, Cross,*" ... and that I, Your poor child, do not die to give You my gifts!

Tell me that I do not guess Your pain, and that my tears do not cry over it, eaten away by Your sorrows.

Tell me that we both do not burn at the same time with the same desires... with equal pain, for the same ideal! Tell me that the Tabernacle is not my delight, the subject of my envy, and that I do not live inside of it, leaning upon Your most pure chest, looking for Your glances of holy fire, just as the moth looks for light! Tell me that I do not burn there, remaining just like a poor worm of the earth!

Tell me that I do not desire everything that has something to do with You, everything that is close to You!

Tell me that those eyes that are always looking at me do not make me happy; that I do not wish to drown myself and be lost in tenderness in the depth of those eyes that are always blessing!

Tell me that Your Heart is not my light, my life, my love!

Tell me, Jesus, if with such intimacy I do not love You with divine passion, with frenzy, with detachment — O, yes, with trust!

And finally, tell me if Your Cross is not my Cross, if Your sacrifice is not my own, if that bed is not my delight, if that Calvary is not MY EVERYTHING!

O yes! Yes! And tell me, above all, instead of my having to say it to You, Jesus, my Jesus and my Delight, tell *me* that I *do* love You, and that is *how* I love You — what I tell You of the ardor of my love is not enough — I have accepted a total destruction of my own nature, so that You may reign, so that You may triumph, and so that You may be glorified!

Do You see how much I love You?

With Your help, I have told You this, but now I say, "Blood for blood... Life for life... Cross for cross... and Love for love!"

RESPONSE

This entire Holy Hour has been a response, Jesus of all my soul! How could I name it? What name can I give it? An *Hour of Heaven*? No, because in heaven You are not present as in the Sacrament. An *Hour of the Angels*? No, my Jesus, because the angels do not need to speak to You as I do, from heart to Heart, and are not able to do it in this manner, because they are spirits. Can it be an *Hour of the Eucharist*... an *Hour of Love*... an *Hour of Jesus,* an *Hour of Both of Us*? O, yes, an *Hour of Both of Us*, because in it, *my Beloved has been completely mine and I have been completely my Beloved's.*

Is it not true, my Mother, that I am completely and only His own and forever His?

6

HOLY HOUR

Mary and the Eucharist

Spiritual Setting: Let us see the most pure and humble Mary, who, presenting Jesus in her arms to us, says: "Look, my child, be like me — pure... be like Him, a victim, like this Jesus Who loves you so."

Petition: Today we shall ask Jesus to be like Him, always a victim, with the purity and whiteness of Mary.

Response: Let us become living hosts, in the sacrifice which pleases Him, through pure love, without tarnishing our souls with the smallest speck.

Mary was a perfect living Cross, and that is the reason she could give us a fruit more precious than any other fruit, an Immaculate Jesus, pure, divine, holy... Lily from lily, Iris from iris.

This is the reason for the intimate likeness between Mary and the Eucharist, this marvelous union.

The Eucharist always reminds me of Mary, and Mary reminds me of the Eucharist.

That divine Flesh, that most pure Blood that is presented to us in the Sacrament of Love, I owe primarily to Mary.... Before being born upon the altars, He was born in Mary.... Mary's bosom was the first one to receive the Body of God, and her hands the first ones to touch Him.

Mary was the first altar, the first priest and a victim in intimate and perfect union with the divine Word.

The cave in Bethlehem, where Mary laid my Child Jesus, was the first of all the tabernacles... and the poor clothes that wrapped Him were the first corporals. O, my God, how could I approach the Eucharist, how could I receive it in my heart without thinking about Mary? To whom is it that I owe that treasure of my soul, that divine life, the seed of purity for my heart, if not through the Eucharist given through Mary?

To whom, then, will I ask for love, for an ardent love, pure, immense, and unequaled? Who, if not Mary, can teach me to love and also to sacrifice myself?

O, Mary, Mary! How I envy your joy when you embraced Jesus against your heart and in your arms! How I envy the sweet moments you spent with Him, and above all, *what you did to please Him*! My heart is never clean enough and my soul is always stained.... What did you do, Holy Virgin, to please Him? How did you caress Him? With what fervor did you receive Him?

Second Meditation

"I received Him, my child, being His servant... and as such, I kissed His feet.... I received Him as His mother, and then I kissed His forehead.... I received Him as a daughter and then I kissed His hands... but always humbling myself... always disappearing so that He could appear in me. I received Him with an ardent thirst to possess Him.... I received Him with the whiteness of the lily of the valley in my heart... with the fire of more than a million Seraphim... with greater purity than that of all the angels, and with a deeper suffering than that of all the martyrs."

But, with pain, Mother of the soul, why?

"Pain because of the insults that He received… because of the forgetfulness of souls… because of the ingratitude of His own people… because of a longing to possess Him that was killing me.

"And thus is the preparation you need to receive Him; you must be humble, pure, mindless of yourself, ardent and with suffering and reparation, and with the martyrdom of desiring to possess Him forever."

Yes, pure, Virgin, we promise this, but help us; lend us your heart with all its feelings so that we can approach the Loved One. Every morning we think of you in a very special way, beloved Mother. At the foot of the altar when we see the Lord come out of His tabernacle, when we feel ourselves enveloped in His radiance, when the bell tells us we are not worthy to receive Jesus in our hearts. O, Mary! Then our souls fly to you, asking for your purity, your fire, your hunger, your celestial ardor with which to love — Ah! He Who is LOVE.

With your own substance you fed that Eucharistic Jesus Who is going to give me life; and I, when I receive Him, transported by my joy, I in a certain way receive your virginal milk, your most pure blood, your whiteness, Mother, feeling that I really am your child!

O, yes, my God! Mary and the Eucharist,

the Eucharist and Mary, are the most cherished delights of my life, the most beloved objects of my heart. They teach me to be pure.... They show me the Cross, inviting me to be a victim in their union. But if Mary teaches me charity... she tells me to forget myself, to give myself to others, to be like her, *all for everyone* without exception... that I live hidden, in darkness, poor, obedient, maybe despised, but always doing good with a pure love, to please the heavenly Father!

"What do you say, my soul? From now on will you be a faithful copy of Mary and of the Eucharist? Be pure, always pure; this is the only way to become a Host, to be saintly, to be a victim!"

THIRD MEDITATION

I will be so. With God's grace I shall be pure and victim. That Eucharist, which is all my love, ignites me.

Here at the foot of the tabernacle I have an intimacy with this Jesus Host that the world does not see or understand, or realize, because it is so pure.... Here, without witnesses, without noise and without the world... the caresses and the tenderness, the suffering and the tears flow.

Here, Jesus, my sighs burn You and Your

gazes scorch me… here I hand my suffering over to You, and Your love envelops me…. Here, at the foot of Your tabernacle my heart explodes through the fire which consumes it, and the ardent lava of this volcano changes into madness, into compressed tenderness, into suffocated delirium…; I tell You this here — is it not so, my Lord? My sorrow and my pain, my sin and miseries… we mutually dry the tears of our souls, and, O! The world is ignorant of what the angels contemplate: the abasement of the Word made nourishment… of a Jesus three times saint and a thousand times *loving!*

O My most beloved Eucharist! Here I tell You my sorrows and You help me to endure them, sweetening them with Your nearness.

And my love grows in proportion to my emptiness, to my abasement, to my losing myself in my filthiness and in my naught… but how can I be a victim, how can I love You more, my Jesus?

"Whenever you sacrifice yourself willingly for My sake… whenever you hide so I may appear… whenever you are nothing so I may be everything.

"You will love Me more, much more, child of My Heart, when you sacrifice everything that is not I… when you renounce being anything that is not rubbish… when you dim yourself so others may shine, when you faithfully guard the whiteness of your soul, when you sacrifice your-self in silence and obscurity *only to please Me.*"

I promise You, my Eucharistic Jesus, only because I love You, to unite all the blood of my heart — all of its affections and all my love — with Your Heart. You are the outstanding passion of my soul, my constant thought.... Your Blood flows through my veins and You are the breath of my life, the Lord of my whole being.

O, my Heaven, my Life, my Jesus! What can be more my own than Mary and You in the Eucharist?

Response

O, Mary of my soul, our beloved Queen! Jesus is going to make a victim out of me, but you are going to give me your very purity. "Like the lily among thorns are you, Mother among the daughters of Zion" — which is to say that you exceed all of them with your incomparable purity. Many souls have followed you, Mary, in the pure path of virginity... many of them have acquired your lily whiteness, but not one of them has been able to deny this about herself: "I have been originated in iniquity; my mother begot me in sin." Only you, Mary — Immaculate in your Conception, Immaculate in your divine maternity, Immaculate in your life and in your death!

If the angel directs you from the beginning, announcing the Mystery of the Incarnation, this does not surprise me, because you are the Virgin par excellence.... If God Himself lovingly contemplates the humility of His hand-maid, this does not surprise me, because you are Mary, like the lily in the depth of the valley.

How much do I rejoice that you, exalted Virgin, are queen of this chaste and pure generation, which crucified and fed with the Eucharist will establish its dwelling place in heaven!

The lily of the fields is more splendid than Solomon in his glory, but the lily of heaven and of our hearts is Mary.

O, most beloved Mother! Give us purity and love, whiteness and the Eucharist. Amen.

7

HOLY HOUR

Thoughts

Spiritual Setting: To see Jesus today, Who very lovingly descends from the monstrance and setting His holy hand upon my forehead, says to me in an entreating tone: "Are you going to give Me what I will ask of you? There are still many things lacking before you are totally Mine."

Petition: We shall ask the Lord the grace of completely belonging to Him, without losing an atom of perfection.

Response: Begin today to completely belong to Jesus, in thoughts, words, and actions.

"My child, since I chose you from all eternity, I have enveloped you in very special graces.... And for what? Only for your own good and for My glory... solely to make you happy by reflecting Myself in your whole being... solely to transform you in Myself, making you a living image of your Beloved Crucified.

"My child, I desire that whoever looks for you will find Jesus in your place... and this *always... everywhere... and no matter who it is.*

"How I would like to see you that way! Your body torn apart, like Mine... your soul desolate and forsaken, like My soul... your heart, completely My own, pierced by the lance... pricked with thorns... scorched with all its tenderness, with all its compassion, with all its fire, always a victim, child of My soul.

"As a victim! For what? So that our union may be more binding... so that human frailty, with all its deformity, may die... your self-indulgence, your ego which makes war against your perfection... so that then the life-giving and creative gaze of My Father might rest upon you. What do you say to this? Will I obtain it? How will you respond?"

No, Jesus of all my being! I am not worthy.... Do not say that! I wish only to sink... to press myself against the earth and strike my breast, only crying for my sins and asking You for pardon.... But Your love draws me.... Lord! Lord! I am Yours and I always will be Your own. What is it that You desire — what?

Second Meditation

"My child, I desire all of *your thoughts* to always be Mine. The thoughts of man are generally very suspicious, and from grace's viewpoint, how few of them are without flaw!

"I am going to give you a precious rule which will keep your mind forever pure; practice it, My child, so that I will come to your aid. It is this: Try to think inside of your Jesus; do not just live, but *think* with My very thoughts, so saintly, so immaculate, and as transparent as the sky without clouds, so divine.

"Think very often: 'In this case, how would Jesus think?' And think how I would think, that is, always with purity, always with zeal and charity.

"Every time that you realize that your thoughts have escaped from their place, from the interior of your Jesus, and from Mary's side, bring them back, child, sweetly and softly toward Me; this will not be easy for you at first; but if you work at it, you will attain it, until, without even noticing, you will do this every moment of your life.

"Think then, from now on, only about Me and in everything *inside of Me.* Am I not your dwelling place, your temple, your chamber, your cloister, in the end, even when you are not religious?

"Do you need to go out to the streets and the public places to think? No, think wherever you are. And if I am your life, where, then, will you think? In this manner little by little you will draw the figure of your Jesus into yourself, profoundly hidden in Him.

"I am your sea, and I want you to be a shell that lives hidden in its depth, pure and clean, hiding its pearl. Live in this manner, pure and clean, even more so than the water, hiding your thoughts and drowning them in the waters of this sea. Do you promise Me this today?"

THIRD MEDITATION

"But, do you know to which sea I am referring? … To the sea of blood and bitterness… to the shoreless sea of loving fire that exists in the depths of My Heart. That is where I want the shell about which I told you, clean and pure in all its thoughts, and as transparent as crystal. My child, that is where you bind yourself as the shell, with your Pearl — Jesus…. There you will press it, you will encrust it within yourself, and

Jesus and you, you and Jesus will come to be only one.

"All your thoughts will be *bleached*… will be *divinized*… will be *transformed*.

"In that sea of My Heart, in the close contact of your Pearl, and drenched as a sponge in its blood and in its fire.

"My dearest child, put these rules into practice. I will demand an account of them some day, which might not be far off, so that from now on your thoughts do not belong to you, they are Mine, soaked in My *substance*… in My *memory*… in My *love*.… In this manner these thoughts cannot be other than saintly, just, and non-judgmental; these thoughts cannot make less charitable conjectures against your neighbor; without prejudice or erroneous rash judgments — seizing form and life in Me, all of them directed to My greatest glory.

"This is what I expect of you… this is the gift that My Heart asks of you today. Will you give it to Me? Or do you prefer to soil your forehead — which should only have the reflection of Myself — with the world: worldliness, vanity, jealousy, envy, pride, vengeance, and so on — as this is where these passions form themselves trying to corrupt the heart?

"O, no! This is not what I expect of you as payment for the tenderness and goodness with which I have constantly enveloped My children.

Today, during these moments, I will take and divinize all of these minds and all of these thoughts."

RESPONSE

O Jesus, Jesus of all my heart, of my soul, of all my life! You, only You, will be the Jesus of my thoughts, and my thoughts will be like the thoughts of my Jesus.

Yes, I promise this, my Lord, because what in the world or in any place, is there that can attract my thought, that can fix my thought and captivate it, but You, my Treasure, my sweetest Jesus, so pure, so beautiful and saintly, You Who fill everything that enchants it, that divinizes it and makes everything delightful? Why not think only about You, so white... so pure... so sweet and divine, so full of sincerity, so heavenly?

Certainly your charms attract me, Jesus! Your smiles enrapture me! Your tenderness mesmerizes me! Your gaze, so divine, celestial and profound, inflames and carries me away.... Your Heart scorches me, Your Blood inebriates me, and Your Cross, O my Jesus, Your Cross is my delirium, my happiness, my passion and my life! And if all of this is my breath, my milieu, My warmth, how then can I think about what is not my constant thought?

If You are my heaven, my treasure and the only love of my life, Who puts all my other earthly loves at Your feet, how could I refuse to give You all my thoughts? O, no, my Jesus, You know it! Certainly I am vileness itself, the filthiest mud: but O, my Immaculate Lily! From now on I will *erase myself* from the world, and I will forever keep my mind inside of my Pearl Jesus.

Mary Immaculate! Give me the purity of your thoughts so I can reflect Jesus in them. Amen.

8

HOLY HOUR

He Hides Himself to Come Nearer to Us

Spiritual Setting: Let us contemplate the Lord hidden in the Eucharist, Who, showing Himself through the sacred veils, says to each one of us: "If I abase Myself it is to come nearer to you, O soul whom I so love!"

Petition: Today, with our whole heart and soul, we will ask our dearest Eucharist for the unequaled grace of a humble anonymity, so that we may be able to come near to Him.

Response: During this week we shall practice multiple acts of humility and silence, the only means to attain anonymity.

"My child, I dwelled in the depths of the heavens, but seeing you through the centuries, *with a gaze* that was wrapped in an infinite love, and with the tenderness of a God, I said to Myself, *My children are alone.... I am very far away from them... but I will come down.... I will minimize Myself to come near to them.... I will descend, hiding My splendors and My glory so as not to dazzle them.... I will come nearer and nearer, and then these children will be ALL MINE and at the same time, I will BE ALL THEIRS.*

"The angels are admired... hell roars... but the Word becomes incarnate.

"This first step that united you to Me, My child, was not enough for My love.... I thought about you from all eternity, but I desired to live at your side... to become your brother... to carry within Me, dear child, the same blood as your own! And what did it matter if I had to dull the rays of My Divinity if I would come closer to you?

"And this is why I made Myself man: because this bond was even tighter, because this union enclosed greater delights for My Heart. If My Divinity alone had come near to you, your eyes would have been dazzled and blinded with the gleams of My light, but becoming incarnate in Mary, you would be able to contemplate Me without fear, and feel My hands that would press you... my feet tired from following you... and you would contemplate My Cross and a Heart like yours, burning with love for you, nailed upon it.

"What do you say, dearest child? Are you moved by the infinite fire of My love?"

Surely, Jesus of my soul! Look my Lord! Contemplating You in Bethlehem or sleeping upon Mary's knees, I see You smaller than in Your highest creation; but I LOVE YOU EVEN MORE... working at Nazareth, You seem smaller than when creating the world, and because of this I LOVE YOU MORE.

Served by Martha You seem smaller than living in heaven served by the angels and the Seraphim, and so I LOVE YOU MORE.... Sad and dying upon the Cross You seem smaller than reigning with the Father and the Holy Spirit through the ages, and because of this I DO LOVE YOU SO MUCH MORE, dear Jesus, adored and blessed Jesus! O, how could I not love He Who Is Love itself?

Second Meditation

"I was profoundly hidden in the Incarnation, but it still was not enough.... How could I hide Myself even more? My flesh was already similar to your own flesh, but how could I live nearer to you … hiding Myself under the appearance of bread, and making Myself even smaller than under the likeness of man? And this other intimate bond that I was yet going to contract with you in the Eucharist would bring Me even nearer to you, so that I would constantly be at your side, day and night.

"That is why, burning with love, on the night that preceded My Passion, I said, *'Take and eat, this is My Body…. Take and drink… this is My Blood,'* because I thought of you, because I foresaw this day, when you would be here at the foot of My throne contemplating Me.

"My mortal life had been enclosed within the short span of thirty three years, but My Eucharistic life would last as long as the world exists. In those times very few people knew Me, but in the Eucharist all generations to come will find Me on the Altar, always blessing; always loving!

"Being God as I am, I was not unaware of the outrages and sacrileges, all of the hatred for which I would be a target; but what could this matter to My love, if My pleasure was to be always *to hide Myself in order to come nearer to you,* to dry the tears of My children, to live with you under the same roof, to breathe the air which you breathe, to be your companion and your life, your comfort and your all? One would say that the Eucharist is a deep night, My child, but no, it is not so, it is the splendor of the Father that shines in the midst of the sweetest delights.... One would say it is the most impenetrable silence, and nevertheless, it is the eternal Word, sweeter than honey! One would say it is the greatest inaction and death, and it is the activity and the life... it is Life, child, the eternal Life which you must breathe, because it is purity... it is saintly... it is profound in the grace and virtue that will lead you to perfection.

"Child of My Soul, I am in the Eucharist so that I can live more intimately with you... to be your comfort, your father, your friend, your solace, your heaven upon earth.... It is My love that compels Me to cover Myself with these veils... to keep the secret of My glory.

"*'Goodness appeared upon the earth'*... and goodness continues in the Eucharist, attracting souls by its gaze... by His love... breathing at the ear of every soul with indescribable sighs that set one on fire and that purify... but is My love yet satisfied?

"Think and guess, child of My Heart, what else was needed for Me to further abase Myself, to further hide Myself?"

THIRD MEDITATION

What is this *"further,"* Jesus of my soul? Where could You minimize Yourself even more than in a consecrated Host?

"In your heart, My dearest child, in your heart; and this is the last step to which the Incarnate Word descends, it is there where I hide to work marvels in your favor; in that solitary and narrow throne I repose to transform it, to do it good, by communicating the holy fire to it, with My own substance.

"I come down happy and content to your heart to give you peace… to make suffering easy for you… to form in you a *Cross* upon which I can rest.

"Tell Me, dear child, before having known and tasted the Eucharist, what did you really know? And after you have become familiar with it, what do you ignore? After inebriating yourself with this wine that engenders virgins, did you know all of the delights of purity and chastity? Before having been fed with this mysterious bread in which I abase Myself, did you know perfect humility? Before having united yourself with the Divine Victim of Calvary, did you know true patience? Before having participated in love's feast, before knowing Me, child of My Soul, did you know charity? And after the Eucharist becomes your customary food, what do you ignore about the sublime ways through which the souls of saints elevate themselves from virtue to virtue?

"Look, My child: Baptism makes Christians, Confirmation makes Christians perfect, but *only the Eucharist makes saints.*

"When you receive the Eucharist you become one with Me, another Jesus; but do you show this in your thoughts, in your words, and in your works? Do you reproduce Me in yourself, being humble, patient, sweet, attractive, self-sacrificing, obedient, silent and pure? This must be the effect of My intimacy and union with you… this is why I remain in the Eucharist… and descending all of these steps, I have finally arrived at My final approach toward you to take possession of your heart.

"The world may say, 'Goodness has newly appeared. Jesus lives, Jesus dwells, Jesus acts, shining through loving children, reproducing in them *His life as victim, His zeal for souls, His thirst for suffering,* His incomparable love for the Cross.'

"If this is not so, I will again enclose Myself in the tabernacle with tears in My eyes, with pricking thorns in My Heart.

"'*It is no longer I who lives now, but You in me.*' Can you say this to Me, dear child, or at least truly offer it to Me? Say yes, because our time is coming to an end; offer to imitate Me this week, hiding from everything in order to come near to Me, descending to find Me no matter what; this is what your Jesus Host, your Jesus Word, your Jesus Victim desires of you."

RESPONSE

What can I say? Jesus, Jesus, what can I offer You, with all my soul, with all my heart, but to render myself into Your divine arms without reserve, and hide myself, conceal myself, and fly away from myself and from all self-will, to FIND YOU, Jesus of my soul? You have overcome infinite distances with the light and the strength of Your love, to find me and to unite Yourself to me, poor and filthy mud! And I, Lord, will I not bulldoze everything, giving blood and life to find You?

If You hide and descend to find me, dear Jesus, I will also hide myself in interior silence, and will humble myself without measure to come near to You: this is the way to become united to You. From now on, my heart will be the cradle where You repose, the workshop where You labor... the Calvary where You immolate Yourself. I will be Your sepulcher, Your nest, Your tabernacle, Your monstrance, Your ciborium, YOUR HEAVEN.... O, Lord, Lord! A rubbish dump — Your heaven? Yes, Your clean, pure sky studded with the stars of all the virtues.

Forgive my delirium, my passion, my madness, *but it is love, my Lord, which makes me desire to give You what I do not have, everything I would like to have…* but this Eucharist steals my heart and my senses, O hidden God, concealed God, loving God! O mysterious food that unites me to Him Who is my life! Grant me that when You abase Yourself in me, Jesus, I may be reborn in You, and that when I disappear You may appear in every one of my actions, reproducing Yourself, for this is what a child of Your Heart must be.

My Mother, harvested little violet from Nazareth, hide me within your Immaculate Heart. Amen.

9

HOLY HOUR

Treasure

Spiritual Setting: I shall contemplate Jesus, resplendent in the midst of a thousand rays of light, in the attitude of the Ascension, opening His chest and pointing to His burning Heart, with its Cross, saying to me: "Here you have your treasure... *and here is where I want to have My own treasure.*"

Petition: O, Lord, grant me the grace that I no longer think, nor want, nor look for any treasure other than Your Heart.

Response: I will spend this entire week in internal seclusion, enjoying my only treasure, emptying myself of "I," and filling myself with Him.

Jesus of my soul, Eucharistic Jesus, Jesus Victim. *You are my treasure!* But so the world and its creatures do not steal You from my arms, today I am going to hide You deep in my heart.… Here, silent and secluded, I will joyfully contemplate You, being happy in the possession of a Heaven … and this is what You *are for me,* adorable Jesus, a Heaven upon earth… an oasis in my exile… the richness of riches, the All of my heart.… I dream about You, Jesus, in Your complete possession, in Your crucified love that can make me a victim with You. What greater joy, Lord, than to die to myself at every instant in order to possess You in the fullness of our union? There is nothing, nor is there anyone who can snatch from my arms the Treasure that my soul has chosen — is that not true?

"Child, no one will be able to take you away from Me except sin; but among My devoted souls, could such a monster ever exist? O no, because they would cease to be My comfort… the solace of your Jesus.

"I certainly am your only Treasure, My child, your rich Treasure that never declines nor grows old.

"My Heart is a Treasure disclosed to the world… but the Cross of this Heart that I am showing you is a chosen and hidden Treasure…

it is the Treasure of treasures, it is the Treasure that I want to give to you.... I, with My Heart, and with its Cross, am a triple Treasure.... What else can you desire, My beloved child, if they are the jewels from heaven, of the Holy Spirit and of the Father, the same ones that you will contemplate during your meditation hours?

"I, your Jesus, am a Treasure of graces and of infinite perfections.... I am a Treasure of love... a Treasure of suffering... of virtue... of teachings... of tenderness... of charm... of *anything you could desire*, My child, of anything you desire, and in Me you can quench your thirst. Satisfy your hunger by making Me *completely yours.*

"Call Me in this manner: *your Treasure, your Treasure!* But imitate Me... unite yourself to Me... and be My portrait... and be My spouse... and be My Cross.... Will you grant Me this?"

Lord, Lord! What can my poor heart refuse You? What can I desire except to belong completely to You and to be abandoned to Your Will? O my Treasure, allow me to lose myself in Your presence, seized by Your tenderness and ravaged by Your love.

"I have already heard you, child of My Heart... but today I am going to ask you for something that you cannot deny Me.

"I desire you to be My treasure.... If I am your Treasure, why is it that you may not be My treasure?"

Me, my Jesus.... Me, Your treasure? But what is this I hear? Is this possible? Is it a dream? ... Is it madness or confusion?

I, a treasure, and Yours... and of what? A treasure of filthiness... of pride... of self-reliance... of envy... of laziness... of jealousy... and trash! O Jesus, Jesus! And, why do You embarrass me and make me blush from confusion?

You, my Life, Who fashions the brilliant stars and the angels, and Who are the owner and creator of the stars, do You want me, O my God, to be Your treasure?

"Do not be frightened.... I do not tell you that you *are* My treasure, but that *I want you to be My treasure;* and even without these words I have asked you to be so many times, when I asked you *to be My Cross.*

"O child of My sorrows and of My love... *Listen*: What else can it mean to be My treasure but *to be My Cross?*

"The Cross is and always has been the treasure of your Jesus... the hope of the Father...

the triumph of the Holy Spirit. And to be the treasure of the Trinity, it is enough to be My Cross… and loving souls will be My treasures if they are My Cross.

"And why is it that I want them to be My Cross? So they may frighten away Satan, who flees even at the shadow of the Cross."

Why, then, is it that he comes to frighten us, my Jesus?

"Perhaps because these crosses are not perfectly formed."

Well, then, fashion me at Your pleasure, please. Your Cross was pierced, full of blood — stains, upright, and with a lily nailed upon it.… I will then stretch out my arms to the nails of self-crucifixion, and desire to have that Lily nailed upon me, and to never be separated from Him.… Then I will truly be Your treasure, because I will bear within myself the Treasure of treasures, the triple Treasure. Come now, Jesus, come, come, I will not leave this place until this is done.

Third Meditation

"I certainly do desire for you to be My treasure, but a treasure hidden within My Heart.… Do you not know that there is your dwelling place, your true retreat, *inside* of your Jesus? Don't you recall this Cross that lives hidden in the depths of My Heart, barely seen? Do you not know that your life must run its course silently and pure… recollected and even absorbed by interior solitude and in the presence of the Loved One?

"When will you understand that your place, beloved child, is here in the depths of this Heart that permitted itself to be opened by a lance so that you could enter… and lose yourself in it?

"Today, during these moments, throw yourself into the wound at My side and the one in My Heart, entering to transform yourself into the treasure of your Jesus with the intimate and constant union with its hidden Cross, sweetening its bitterness… softening its roughness… lightening its weight… by your purity… by your self-denial… with your love."

RESPONSE

Lord of my soul, of my life, of my entire being, of my existence, of all my love! You ask for *purity, abandonment,* and *affection?* What would my love not give You and what would I not renounce in order to sweeten, to soothe, and to take away the weight that oppresses Your Heart, giving it consolation? During this week I promise You to uproot my ego and trample it… to keep the purity of my soul intact and not to lose sight of You, keeping Your divine presence always and everywhere without dissipation. I want to transform myself into a Cross because in so many ways You are demanding it from me, Beloved of my soul.... I want to live and die hidden in a sacrifice which borders on immolation, *very far away from every human glance*, burning myself like incense in the midst of my roughness, with a constant death to all self-will.... Help me, my Life, to *destroy* within my heart every self-indulgence, consuming myself *silently* as the candle before Your altar.

Jesus of my soul, Treasure of my life! May I finally be Your Cross, but a Cross hidden beneath the soil everyone tramples... an ignored and scorned Cross at least... a Cross that drives away all enemies... a Cross that may attract the gazes of the Father... a Cross that stops the avenging justice upon the poor sinners... a Cross that stands in the way of souls that are rolling into hell... a Cross that makes purity blossom... a Cross that at last encounters all the conditions — even if pierced and blood-stained — to truly be the Treasure of Jesus, His real comfort, planted and always fresh and full of flowers and the fruits of virtue, within the BLOOD OF YOUR MOST SACRED HEART.

O Mary, Jesus's first treasure! Make us saintly, teaching us to suffer for love's sake. Amen.

10

HOLY HOUR

Love

Spiritual Setting: To see Jesus Who says to me from that beloved monstrance, "Come, beloved child, come near to the Heart that loves you so and *listen… listen…* because love's perfection consists in listening, more than in speaking… in working more than in feeling."

Petition: Love for the hidden life, for being forgotten, for obscurity and humiliation, *loving.*

Response: To assimilate myself with Jesus today, in the lovable silence of His tabernacle, carrying Him all day long in my heart, contemplating Him… listening to Him… dying of love for Him.

The Lord speaks: "Your soul, My child, is very dear to Me, and I Myself am going to form it for My solace, giving it the form of the Cross.

"Do you not feel My eyes fixed on you?

"Do not My gazes make you shiver, when they wrap you in love, purifying your heart?

"I come today to invite you to follow Me.... *I want you to fall in love with Me*, because once this first step is taken, nothing will be difficult for you, and you will spread your wings toward Calvary.

"Enter... today enter into this open Heart that loves you so. Do you not see it full of fire? It burns to convey the fire to you. Do you not see it full of light? This is to illumine your path toward suffering.

"In it you will find everything you need... fortitude... purity... humility... and everything you desire, as it is the fountain of every good.

"Do not fear, and enjoy, My child, and plunge yourself into this sea of indescribable delight, unknown to the world.

"Drown yourself inside of your Jesus... and once you are satisfied, and soaked there a thousand times, then, O soul so deeply loved by Me! Then you will have barely touched the sweetness of the Heavenly Spouse with your lips!"

"Do you desire My union with you? I must warn you that you will never find disappointment in this union, but certainly *many thorns and many crosses...* but, My child! These are the pearls which your Beloved One is going to give you, and promise Me that you will never lose heart.

"You have to hug the Cross... to *press it* against your breast... and it will yield a *delightful juice...* I promise you this, if you love suffering... if you are faithful to Me!

"My child... wrap Me in a cloud of love.... I desire to live in you, and what a great honor! Your body will be like Jesus's retreat!

"With this gift your body will be as if dead for everyone else and for yourself, in the sense of not giving itself pleasure... of following its whims... of looking for comfort... and pampering itself.... It is still very lively! Why do you not sacrifice it entirely to Me? If it gets tired, let it be for Jesus... if it conquers itself, let it be for the Lord... if it suffers, what would it matter if My love sweetens your pain?

"What are you going to offer Me today? Tell Me... tell Me, I am already listening to you."

"Yes, My daughter, give yourself entirely up to Me, so I may give Myself entirely to you. If you could only understand how very dear your soul is to My Heart! But work… I want you to be pure, I want you saintly. Prepare yourself for suffering, because if I put you to trial, it shall be according to the measure of strength My grace will give you.

"I am going to ask four things from you today, My child: *Purity, Humility, Trust, and Sacrifice.*

"Your Jesus was absolutely pure unto death, and death upon a Cross.… You must also be pure until death and death upon a cross. Your Jesus was completely humble until death and death upon a Cross.… You must also be completely humble until death, and death upon a cross. O child of My Heart! Why is it that you have so little trust in Me? Why do you not throw yourself into sacrifice without fear? Why do you look for your own interests? Why do those *tiny things* stop you, and why do you not see these open arms that are waiting for you? If you would only understand what is awaiting you! … If you could only know the gift of God! … If you could only measure My love for you!"

Ah, Jesus, my Jesus!

"Yes, My child, I love you… more than you

can guess... and I wish to live with you.... I wish to unite Myself to you; and you do not understand this... and I see that you are stopped by little straws... by silly things... so that it is difficult for you to communicate with Me... with Me, Who does not take My eyes from you, who will not walk if I do not drag you, because it is hard for you to sacrifice yourself. And you still tell Me that you love Me, that you love Me? O no! *Love is not like that!* Here, here in this Heart is where fire burns. How ungrateful you are!"

RESPONSE

O Jesus, Jesus of my life! Do not repeat that word! **Ungrateful!** Look at my tears and see my soul that loves You, *that does love You,* and from now on will love You with all my strength, with all my heart and soul.

I will do everything that You desire, abandoning myself into the hands of my director so he can shape me. No more resistance, my Lord, *yes, I will let myself be shaped* so that I may be Yours forever. I will be Yours, always *humble, obedient and crucified....* I am not ungrateful! O no! This is not possible when one loves You.

Can You not see that just seeing You sad leaves my heart unsettled? And that means that I do not love You? O no, my Jesus, my Sweetness, my Treasure, my Love!

Certainly it is painful to uproot myself from my own being… certainly my self-love still lives in me… certainly it is true that I do not respond to Your graces, that spirit is missing from my actions, that I do not despise myself, nor abhor myself, but O Lord, from this moment on I will tear up my will and my judgment, I will empty my heart of everything that is not You, and with my forehead upon the ground, and even more, with a humble and repentant heart, in a few minutes, when You bless me, I will say: I do love You… yes, I love You… yes, I love You!

O Mary, Mother of Beautiful Love, grant that I may love my Jesus — and yours — more every day! Amen.

11

HOLY HOUR

Agony in the Garden

Spiritual Setting: Let us imagine that we are the rock upon which the agonizing Jesus rested Himself ... the earth that sustained Him, drenched in His Blood.

Petition: We shall ask the Lord, with all our soul, to be deeply touched as we contemplate the Word made flesh in such humiliation.

Response: To wish to love humiliation and *suffering* from now on.

Jesus, my Jesus! What? Is it You, Lord, Whom my soul contemplates... pale... naked... emaciated... alone... abandoned... trembling without being able to hold Yourself upright on Your feet?

Why, my Life, such a sorrow? What is it that causes the agony that I see portrayed on Your face?

"O child! The shame of shames at seeing Myself burdened with all sin in the presence of My Father. This is what My life has been: For these thirty-three years of My life, I have endured, struggled, trying to purify the world... trying to hide that which could not be hidden from My Father's eyes with My innocence and with My *sorrow!*

"Today I can bear no more, and before dying, I want to show future generations, for an instant, the weight that oppressed Me from the moment of the Incarnation, and which the power of Divinity has not allowed to be shown externally.

"My Blood streams down, soaking the earth to purify it.... My soul is sorrowful 'even unto death' and hides itself in this cave, wrapped in the comforting folds of prayer, seeking strength.

"But, look.... I do not have even one heart who can watch with Him Who has consecrated all of His waking moments to save them."

Lord, Lord! Overwhelmed by pain, I fall at Your feet, offering You my arms to hold You up.... How many, many hours of my life have I not stayed up to accompany You, nor have I even thought about You? O how many of them have flown by without my sacrificing my sleep, my pleasures, and my comfort?

I contemplate You *alone* in the Garden of Gethsemane, but even *more alone* in the garden of my heart so dry... so thorny... so icy... so hard... so very full of self. O Jesus, agonizing Jesus! Forgive me, forgive me! From now on this soul does not wish to sleep in its sensuality, but to watch and to love constantly to give You consolation.

SECOND MEDITATION

Jesus perseveres in prayer, but amidst such struggles, desolation, helplessness, and tremendous purification — not for Himself, Who had nothing to be purified of — but for my sins that He was erasing with His Blood until they were all wiped out one by one! ... In addition, giving so many graces, drop by drop, coin by coin, maybe even... to my calling in life!

Jesus suffers deceptions from those He most loved... from those who were His hope and His everything upon earth. In those moments

of supreme anguish no one understood Him...
only His Mother. But she was so far away! With
the weight of solitude, which is so terrible... with
no company except the millions of tremendous
sins which choked Him... with my own sins —
they are so many — which pressed His Heart
with the weight of Divinity, offended with the
ingratitude of thousands of souls that would go
through the world overwhelmed with gifts, but
without knowing or being grateful for a God
abased — because of His love... this, this is what
constituted the greatest martyrdom in the tenderness of His Heart.

And I laughing..., and I sinning..., and I
in vanity, and leisure, and in a bed of roses, de-
spising and even trampling upon — O my God,
the sighs... the tears... the agonies... and the
Blood of the Word Incarnate — Who in silence
and in darkness expiated my crimes and bought
heaven for me!

Is this possible? — *Ingratitude* should be my
name!

THIRD MEDITATION

Every one of these external things embittered
this Lily of Bethlehem, Who would soon be cut
down on Calvary; but that which killed the Heart
that turned inside of His breast, thorn-pricked
and bloodied, which oppressed those delicate

fibers with inexpressible anguish was — yes — to see the Father offended... the Divinity insulted... by blind men forgetting His benefits and voluntarily bringing about their disgrace.... Then, I repeat, some of that cruel but internal martyrdom became obvious, redeeming us through a hidden and silent Cross... which nobody understood, except Mary.

Then Blood began flowing thread by thread, running and soaking that virginal body, even drenching the tunic, and the very earth.... That Blood cried out, "Mercy!" tearing down justice, and thus, Jesus soaked in the price of my redemption... fell to the ground in the excess of suffering, not looking for relief, but to block the entrance to hell with the Word Incarnate and with His arms outstretched in the form of the Cross.

Then heaven and earth shook... and I... what do I do... what do I think... what do I feel... before this heart-rending scene, whose cause is my sins?

I contemplate... deeply moved, I contemplate... terrified... because of my sins... and I weep and my soul is torn to pieces and I do not dare to interrupt that painful scene... that struggle between God and sin... that silence that makes me shiver, because this is an angel's task.

"Drink," the angel says to Him, presenting Him with the cup of all suffering.

"Father," Jesus says, looking up to heaven with His eyes studded with tears, "My Father, if it is possible, let this cup pass from Me to all loving souls; I want to invite them to this agony…. I want them to help Me purchase heaven with this coin of suffering *if it is possible*, that is to say if they are pure, if they love the Cross, if they know the Word and fall in love with Him. If they respond, invite them to drink of this Cup… yet not as I will, but as You will."

This was Jesus' cry of love in the midst of this quintessence of suffering.

"Drink… drink," the angel repeated, placing the Cup on His divine lips… and Jesus thought about those hearts who, in future ages, would suffer with Him for the same cause in a covenant of love that would greatly glorify the Divine Word — and He drank with great longing to the dregs.

And what did this bloodied Lily find? He found the saintly effects of suffering for charity, for love's sake.

He experienced the fortitude that this action communicates in its completeness, and He stood up vigorous and fortified; He quenched His tears, smiled at the Cross and went courageously, content to encounter suffering.

What a lesson! … What charity! … What goals of love!

What shall His children, the children of the

Word Crucified, say to Him today?

Ah, that His Cup may come to us... whatever martyrdom He pleases to send us, that we shall trample after His footprints, that we shall struggle with courage, that we shall die for His glory, transformed into Him through love. Amen.

Response

To be with Jesus and Mary, in the silence of the soul, silence made of love and gratitude.

12

HOLY HOUR

Dove — Heart

Spiritual Setting: We shall see Jesus Who, descending from His Eucharistic throne, approaches us very tenderly… placing His blessed hand upon His Heart, and extending the other one towards us, He tells us with an inconceivable sweetness: "Will you give Me your heart? … I could take it, but no; I want you to give it to Me voluntarily…. Will you give it to Me so that I may go back to My throne with it?"

Petition: We will ask the Lord to take not only our hearts, but everything we have and are, losing ourselves in Him, without finding ourselves again — evermore.

Response: The perfect self-denial and surrender inside our Cloister, our Retreat, Jesus.

"My child! ... My child chosen by your Jesus Who does not cease to fill you with favors! ... Do you want to give Me what I ask you for today? ... *I want you to enter into My Heart.*

"I love you so, soul purified by My Blood, that it is not enough for Me to have you near Me, look at you.... I need you to be inside of Me... so near to Me, so intimately united to Me, as My own Heart.... You have already entered through the beloved wound at My side... by an inconceivable favor, you are already inside your Jesus, the true Cloister, where all loving souls may enter.

"In this manner, My child, living inside of your Jesus, you will have to live *upon the Cross* — O what a joy!

"The souls that enter inside of Me must be crucified souls.

"This Cloister has many cells, more or less profound.... Choose your own cell, and walk through it hand in hand with Mary, My Holy Mother... transforming yourself... until you arrive not only at those surrounding My Heart, but at the Heart itself, the center of fire, of graces, and of light, transforming you.

"I want you to be there, hidden... silent... anonymous... drinking... absorbing its substance... living from its life....

"That is the waiting room to heaven... that is heaven itself... that is infinite LOVE.

"My child, do you accept? ... Will you let yourself be formed? ... Will you live in that same Heart, with its own tendencies? ... With its same charity? ... With its same virtues? ... With its same loving fire, ignited to a million degrees by SUFFERING?

"O yes, beloved soul: tell Me you are willing... tell Me that from now on and without delay, you are going to learn to be *humble*... to be *pure*... to be *crucified* so as to assimilate yourself to Me. What do you answer Me? I want an *explosion of love*, with very firm purposes of mending your ways."

Second Meditation

"But, so as to come to live inside of My Heart, you have to go through your Cloister, Jesus... the interior of your Jesus, where the fire of My Heart is very lively.... There, inside of Jesus Crucified, you sometimes will find darkness, rugged passages... stumbling and dryness... but do not fear; ...such *is the interior life in its greater part*.... Nevertheless, as I told you, heat will not be lacking there... the flames which burn My Heart on the outside, and more so internally, will bring light to illuminate at the right time... and that light that is also fire will illuminate you and make you burn with love, *strengthening you.*

"You will never depart from the Cross, from your Jesus, from My Side; you will live completely hidden and crucified inside of Me... *possessing Me... being made divine through Me.*

"O child of My sorrows, and of My love. You do not realize what it is to live crucified, inside — deeply inside — your Jesus.... There is nothing that can be compared to this, because there one finds peace... true happiness... and a plenitude of LOVE. *This is what I desire for you...* this is what I have in store for the souls that surrender themselves completely to Me.... It seems little for Me to just open Heaven on their account, and to gift them with My complete love... all My Blood and My very Heart so as *to melt them in its very substance.*

"I am ready to hear you.... O tell Me, tell the feelings of your soul... how you are going to respond to Me... how you are going to love Me... I bend toward your breast to listen to your tenderness... what are you going to tell Me? I can guess, My soul; yes, Mine, Mine, more Mine, since I am your Cloister... since you live *inside of My very Being.*"

"I have already heard you… and if your *earthly heart* is moved, My heavenly Heart, although of flesh like yours and sensitive like no other, has also been shaken with delight upon hearing your promises… and seeing your tears of repentance and of love.

"Now truly, dear soul, you shall be all Mine, and My most beloved spouse, even if you are not a religious."

O Jesus of my life! What is this that You are doing? O my God! Why do You humble yourself so?

"I do so because a soul that loves Me attracts Me to such an extent, and no one can surpass Me in mortification and humility.

"Let Me caress your soul. Let Me soothe its wounds.… Have great confidence in Me…, have a great love for Me. See here, I will feed you from My own hands and let you drink from the inside of My Heart, like a little white dove. There I will give you life, *more life*… fire… *more fire*… an immense love even more, *more love*.… I will feed you with My own substance… because I am all yours… because I was born to come near to you… because I died so that even in eternity you would be all Mine… as I stay upon the altars to realize what I am realizing now… as I am your Cross… as I am your Nest! O why, then do you want to escape from My arms… why is it that you fly towards so many things that are not your Jesus?

"I want you to belong completely to your Jesus: you will be His comfort, you will be His Cross, you will be His consolation, you will be His very Heart!"

Response

Jesus, Jesus, my Jesus! What can I say? I am dumbfounded before the heavy weight of Your tenderness! Certainly I have nothing to give You in return except my misery and ingratitude, but also — O yes! — a heart on fire for love of You! Let the world surpass me in everything, except in loving You… but in loving You, never, never!

I love You, my Jesus, in a manner that I love nobody else… more than a brother… more than a friend… more than my parents, more than mothers love their own children, more, much more, a thousand times more! O Jesus, O Heart of my Beloved One! O yes, I love You with such a refined love, so delicate, so grand, so passionate, so unequaled, in such a way that I cannot imagine that there could be a soul that could surpass me in loving You! What a foolish pretension! Look, my Jesus! I love You without any self-interest… with the desire of sacrificing everything for You, without exception…. I love

You with a devouring zeal for Your glory, and I would give all my blood for the sake of seeing You honored with a single act of love offered to You.... I love You with a deep affection, with frenzy... with madness... with an intensity that burns my heart and all of its fibers... with everything it owns and that which it owns not!

I cannot find words, my Jesus, which can express the strength... the greatness... the purity... of the love that I have for You. O Jesus, Jesus of my life... Jesus of all my being! What more can I say to You? That I suffer for not being able to love You more, much more... that I have hope that by living inside Your Heart I will have no other breath than Your own breath to melt myself in Your very martyrdom, in the one Cross, and in the same life!

You have wounded my heart with Your kindness, with Your charm, with Your love.

I feel Your mark, Jesus, my Jesus, in all my soul: here, here I have You, *entire, complete, divine*. O if my heart could be photographed! He would appear... Jesus would appear... Jesus with His arms in the form of the Cross so that I could fall into them...

Jesus, Jesus, Jesus! Forgive the lively bursts of this miserable heart and have pity on me. Mary, my Mother, protect me! Amen.

13

HOLY HOUR

Why Did Jesus Stay in the Eucharist?

Spiritual Setting: Let us see Jesus' gaze really present in that white Host — that irradiating light, tenderness, and kindness penetrates softly down to the bottom of our souls, discovering, we would say, its deepest wounds in order to cure them.

Petition: Let us ask Him, with all the strength of our love, to look upon us… to look upon us with that gaze that makes chosen souls and saints out of us, instilling in us the love for suffering.

Response: A lively presence of God, feeling His gaze wrap us up all day long, as we sacrifice ourselves in union with Him through love.

Tell me, Lord: If Redemption served Your Justice in erasing sin, if with Redemption the distance between man and Divinity — and between earth and heaven — was bridged, why, then, did You perpetuate the sacrifice of the Cross on Your altars? Why did You remain with man to be — O my God! — so insulted?

"Only for love's sake… only for a charitable goal, and from this goal many others resulted.

"I remained upon the altars because of the passionate thirst that consumes the Word made Flesh, Who, might I say, takes pleasure in the sacrifice of Himself for the ungrateful man who despises Him."

What Charity! … Jesus experiences joy in suffering, and I? … Jesus sacrifices Himself for love's sake… and for love of the ungrateful, and I? … Jesus is forgetful of self… and He sacrifices Himself for the souls that despise Him, for the good of those that do not give Him thanks.… and I? It is, nonetheless, my mission… to give myself… to give my works for both good and guilty souls.… It is my duty as a loving child.

Do I do this? With what spirit?

Do I prefer my loved ones, or those who have offended me? … Or do I trust everything to Jesus so that He may use it as He wills?

Have I once stopped myself to think

whether I fulfill this capital point of generosity? Have I procured purity of intention? … Do I recall it often? … Do I examine it… and fulfill the goal of charity which must be the motto of my spirit?

My God! I have so much to be ashamed of!

With my words I say that I sacrifice myself for souls, that I desire to be a victim… but in practice, to which end do I direct all of my works?

Do I perform my works, my activities, my sacrificial life in a supernatural manner? Or do I perform my "oughts" routinely, thus lazily, without stirring up fervor, scattered, and without spirit?

My soul experiences the breadth of Jesus' gaze that bathes me in these moments. Take advantage of these moments of grace, my soul, for if you allow them to pass away, they might never come back again.

Second Meditation

"What do you say to Him, dear child? What is it you are going to offer your Jesus Who looks at you from His throne, awaiting to snatch from you an act of generosity in which you will *give Him everything*, in which you will sacrifice for Him everything you have, in exchange for *His love?*

"How great is your love and the size of your charity, of your tenderness and the sacrifice of your soul towards Him?

"Jesus delighted in sacrificing Himself for you, to buy graces for you, to cure your wounds. … And you?

"Jesus constantly sheds His Blood upon your ingratitude to purify it… and are you less unfaithful, every day more thankful and loving?

"The measure of His love for you *is His Cross* — and what is the measure of your love for Him?

"Do you make Him wait for the response that He asks of you at every moment, or do you fly to encounter sacrifice, just for having the pleasure of presenting Him with a gift? With what intensity do you love Him? With what frequency do you remember Him? … With what hunger do you receive Him? … With what care do you guard the purity of your soul? … With which fire do you sacrifice yourself for Him?

"Which is the brightest virtue of your heart? Which triumphs over yourself do you obtain each day? … How many steps do you descend each day to reach humility?

"To be a true child of the Cross it is necessary to go deep down inside yourself, to deepen your self-knowledge without measure, to spurn and to deny yourself. Do you practice this?

"Contemplate these thoughts deeply, O My

soul, and consider that in spiritual life *everything is great... holy... sublime... and of the greatest importance for heaven."*

THIRD MEDITATION

Lord, Lord! To accomplish my mission of sanctifying myself in my loving commitment, it is necessary that Your gaze not cease to rest upon me, so that my gaze will not depart from You.

I want all my gazes to be wrapped in prayer, confidence and love — a very great love, a gaze that implores, that beseeches, uniting my will with Yours using heavenly bonds that unite my will with Yours.

O my Jesus! Although I do not deserve it, in Your kindness grant me this mutual gaze of love, that my soul never stands away from Your divine presence, that my eyes look for Yours, and always encounter them in order to preserve peace, fortitude and confidence.

Grant that I not look upon the earth or upon worldly things any longer.... I desire only to look upon You, sovereign Beauty, upon this Jesus Who has no equal.

I want to be blinded to every worldly light, which is fleeting and deceitful. I shall follow my Light, Jesus, like the firefly, until I burn inside of it forever.

In the darkness of my nothingness my Beloved will shine, teaching me what a crucified soul must be.

Response

O my Jesus! I have seen my spirit stained by my ingratitude toward You, indifference toward my neighbor, and apathy toward myself. But now, Lord, I am truly repentant, and I LOVE YOU — O yes! — with the lively anxiety of responding to Your goodness, SACRIFICING MYSELF for You, and for everyone else, in union with You!

You are my life, my living and the only delight in my exile! Pluck from my soul, not only my sins, vices and defects, but also every worldly creature that can impede Your LOVE. I pray that pure affections may be diminished, quenched, and extinguished in my soul if they are an obstacle to Your completely filling me.

Eucharistic Jesus! Today, more than ever, I want to consecrate myself to You forever: please be so kind as to accept this poor offering, this miserable victim… through the hands of Mary. I want to be pure, obedient and poor: increase my desires; confirm my promises, which I would defend with all my blood.

I am completely Yours… wanting only what You desire… disappearing completely in my nothingness, despised… forgotten and always doing what is most perfect, without rest… only to please You… and sacrificing myself generously for the sake of souls that please You… loving You ardently day and night, and with all my heart, and with a thousand hearts were I to have them!

O Jesus, Jesus, my Jesus! That is the perfection I wish to attain to help You save souls — yes, sacrificing myself for them up to my last sigh!

O Mary, Refuge of sinners, pray for them and for me. Amen.

14

HOLY HOUR

Jesus' Charms

Spiritual Setting: Let us imagine Jesus leaning upon the Cross, asleep; and without waking Him up, but also without ceasing to look at Him, let us remember His virtues and the kindness of His Heart… and let us consider these three points: How Jesus has been…. How I have been…. How I am supposed to be.

Petition: Lord, give us the light to know You, to fall in love with Your charms more and more, and to see the true state of our deformity and ingratitude.

Response: To love Him Who is LOVE, repairing all of our faults, and *loving* in every moment of our lives.

First Meditation
How Jesus Has Been

Today, my Life, I am going to contemplate You, asleep like this, so as not to disturb Your humility.

True life is to know You, Jesus, and this is why I have come here: to quiet that cry of tremendous tenderness when You told Philip, *"Have I been with you for such a long time and you still do not know Me, Philip?"* This loving cry, which I often hear from the depth of Your Tabernacle, makes me shudder and tremble with love.... Such a long time, truly! And I, I still do not appreciate Your singular affection, Your numberless graces.... I seem to hear what You once said to Father Hoyos: *"Look at Me, Bernardo, for I am completely lovable."*... And I wish to be completely satiated looking at You, but, O Lord, without ever satisfying my love! My eyes often meet Your eyes, but I am ever obliged to lower them in shame.... And You love me, miserable as I am? Like the sun that illumines everything, so does Jesus see everything... and He still allows me in His presence? Yes, He allows me, and even more, today He wishes to enrapture me, *teaching me*. He invites me to examine my conscience: He shall answer it, and I will be confused.

Let us begin. How is Your Heart, Jesus of

my soul? Awaken, or answer in Your sleep, for that Heart always keeps vigil.

"My Heart, My child, did not break a tender stalk, nor quench the smoldering wick. Such is its tenderness!"

And what did You think about, Lord?

"Only about the glory of My Father and about the salvation of souls: *never about Myself.*"

And Your words, my Love?

"They were and are milk and honey, plain and simple: My analogies were not at all pompous or brilliant, but simple and charming: the fig tree, the hen, the birds; 'Look at the birds; they do not sow or reap, they gather nothing into barns, yet your heavenly Father feeds them,' I said. 'The lilies in the field do not work or spin, and they are clothed in a greater splendor than Solomon in all his glory.' I have always been able to relate to the humble of heart."

And Your concern for everyone, my Life?

"My care has always been tender. If I am thrice Holy, I am also *a thousand times a mother*, and I have numbered the hairs of your head, and not one of them shall fall without My willing it."

Will You tell me something about Your humility?

"I always called Myself Son of Man so as to convince you, My child, that I am your brother... that I have your same blood... and during My lifetime, I was compelled to call Myself the Son of God only three times."

And Your kindness, Jesus?

"'Let the little children come to Me, and do not stop them,' I said. By this you will judge if I am kind."

And Your gentleness?

"I passed by and I am in the Eucharist, always pouring out blessings.... I had Zacchaeus come down from the tree and I said to him, 'I wish to dine with you at your home today....' I worked out his conversion and I *was happy* because My joy upon earth is *souls.* I saved the guilty woman. Love has so many resources! I gave water to the Samaritan woman... even when I was burning with thirst.... I saw a widow weep, and I returned her son to her."

And Your gratitude, adorable Jesus?

"I offered an eternal reward for a glass of cold water — even if it was not hot; for the action of the widow who gave her small coins, I promised that the act would be always remembered."

And Your compassion, for which I have such a great need?

"I forgive, My child, and I *forget.* Peter denied Me, and I conferred on him the title 'Prince of the Church....' I appeared to the sinner Magdalene; I toss the sins of those who love Me over My shoulders, so as not to see them... and

I cast them into the sea…. *I dye them with My Blood to whiten them.*

"'Come, come to Me everyone,' I said, 'and I will soothe you…. Ask and you shall receive. You have not asked until now. Knock and it will open for you….' I cried over Jerusalem, and still cry over ungrateful souls, but I always *forget* and *forgive*. FEAR NOT!"

And Your poverty, Lord of my life?

"That was My life. I was hungry and ate kernels of wheat…. I rested My head upon rough nets — the birds have their nests. But I did not have a single tunic, and died naked, with only the nails and the thorns and the Cross touching My body."

And Your obedience, Life of my life, I do not even know what I experience when I contemplate You!

"My obedience? Until death, and death *upon a Cross….* I obeyed Herod and the executioners, and for thirty years I was subject to My parents."

And Your meekness, my Heaven?

"'Learn from Me,' I said, 'for I am meek and humble of heart.' I was silent before the blows, the insults, the slander, and the huge ingratitude of My enemies."

And just let me ask You one last thing, Lord! Forgive me and tell me: And Your love, *Your love*, Jesus of all my soul?

"Ah, My child! The greatest proof of love is giving up one's life, and I did give Mine for you. *'As the Father loves Me, so I also love you,' with God's own love.* This is My desire: 'Father, that as You and I are one, may they all be one with Us.' My children, remain in My love. This is what I most desire, what I have come to look for, especially in religious families: *love, love,* but this does not develop nor grow, except in the soil of humility."

SECOND MEDITATION
How I Have Been

Lord, surrendered through the weight of Your charms... and enamored to folly by Your virtues, I can do nothing else but cry and ask for pardon. My heart is the nest of ingratitude... my thoughts are about everything except about You ... my words are harsh, disdainful, annoyed and hardly charitable.... my humility? O my Lord, I have behaved as if I did not know You... as if I did not live so near to Your Heart... as if I were not Your child... as if I did not bear Your blood and Your life in my soul! What a shame, what confusion! You lower Yourself and I lift myself up... You give to me, and maybe I feel deserving of Your gifts, or at least I do not think about being thankful for them! ... Am I kind, benevolent, compassionate, and grateful? … Do I forgive and forget, and return favor for disdain, not permitting my heart to keep gall within itself?

And my poverty — is it like Yours, Charm of my heart? … And my obedience, is it internal, is it perfect? And my purity, and my love… that love, in what state is it? *How fervent? … To what extent and intensity? … And with what fervor do I offer it to You?*

I am a cesspool of misery, Lord; but from this day on, from this instant, my life shall consist of imitating You, of drawing You into my soul, and furthermore, of absorbing You and capturing Your entire features and resemblance, imitating Your virtues.

Third Meditation
How I Am Supposed to Be

This is how I shall be: very similar to Christ Jesus, meek and humble of heart, patient and resigned, poor and obedient, kind and crucified, in every moment of my life. I will be *grateful* and *humble*, Lord, for the many immense favors that I am very far from deserving, but I will prove my gratitude to You, not only by my words, but with a very delicate and loving response.

O Lord! I have slept on the riches I possess

without recalling that they are *Yours* and that at any time You please, You can take them back to Yourself. I was resting on something that was not mine, except insomuch as I could profit from it. From now on it shall not be so, Jesus of my life; moreover, I will live in fear and trembling of displeasing You, always working and being grateful for Your gifts. I will no longer be ungrateful, Jesus of my soul, and forgive me.

Nor will I build my nest upon what is nothingness, even if it would be Yours, *but not You*.

To love so as to know, and to know so as to love: that shall be my constant occupation. I am lacking intimacy with You, Lord, Who affords me so many graces; empty my spirit of everything which prevents my intimacy with You, so I can live from Your virtues, always deepening them through the constant practice of self-denial. Living life in something that may not be You is brainless, but do not permit it for me: I wish to make my life a tapestry of acts of love that may serve as both cover and life for all my virtues. Give me light, Lord, give me strength, but above all *give me love*, because he who loves flies in the ways of the spirit with the wings of humility and purity.

The hour comes to an end, my Jesus, and I will not leave this place without Your granting me the humility and purity that lead me to love.

Jesus of my soul, ideal of my heart, dream of my life, most tender and sweet Savior! I beg of You to transform me into Yourself, and that I may live and breathe humility and love, sacrifice and love, response and love and so with all the virtues.

To love! This is the constant cry of my spirit — day and night, asleep and awake. "All virtues have no brilliance without love, a covenant cannot be made without love; but to be able to love Me, it is necessary to know Me, study Me, and live within Me to imitate Me."

This is what I want, Jesus, and for this my soul ardently thirsts! Today, then, today, this very instant, let this celestial fire burn me, set me on fire, and melt the ice in which I am congealed! Scorch me and make this miserable heart turn into ashes. Give it to me, Lord; pluck it from Your breast so that it may consume Your poor and guilty child.

Mary, Mary! I want to be your poor little beggar of love. Amen.

15

HOLY HOUR

Tears

Spiritual Setting: We shall see Jesus, Who from His monstrance extends His hands toward us. With His eyes full of tears, He presents a golden chalice to each one of us, saying, "Will you give Me your tears, child of My Heart?"

Petition: Today we shall ask the Lord for a great generosity to sacrifice, without resisting the dispositions of His Will.

Response: To seal our lips during this week to the least word of complaint, silently sacrificing our hearts through love.

"Today, My child, I come to ask you for your tears.... I want them, My beloved child, to calm My thirst."

Jesus, Jesus of my soul! What are You saying? What have I heard? Your tenderness is inconceivable, Beloved Master of my heart. But what do You want them for, if You are the very essence of them, that is, the font from which they spring, my whole life? ... My tears are not like those pearls that spring from Your eyes, and I am ashamed to offer them up to You.

"In a mystical sense I understand this, My child... and if they spring only out of love or of pain, believe Me, they will soothe the thirst of My Heart which is looking for tenderness... *it burns with the desire for crucified souls.*

"And where would I look for this except within the souls that are prepared to burn in love and in sacrifice? ... Have you traced your conduct on silent, patient, and resigned sacrifice? Have you offered Me your suffering, smiling and abandoning yourself to My Will? ... If you have shed some tears, have they been born of My love, or of humble and self-denied sorrow? What do you answer Me? My kindness, child, permits sorrows for your good..., and if your tears are My comfort... if they sweeten My bitterness, will you complain about the causes that brought them about, forming with them, moreover, an immortal crown that you will soon wear?

"If this is so, it is certain that you do not love Me, or that your love for One who loves you so much is very weak... for He Who has wept so much to purchase graces for you... for Him Who still cries because of your limited perfection and your ingratitude! What do you say? What do you respond? What do you promise Me in these moments during which, with My eyes drenched in tears, *I remind you of My tenderness... My favors... My blood ... and My love?"*

SECOND MEDITATION

"There are two kinds of tears, My child. Some are of no value and the others are pearls for Me, which I collect in this golden chalice that I hold in My hands and which My children must fill.

"There are some tears that are merely external, and come only from the eyes and there are deeply internal tears from the heart, that are brought forth sometimes by love, or sometimes by sorrow. These tears of the soul are of blood, and they are pleasing to Me.

"Tears from the eyes, child, spring forth for a thousand reasons that have no merit for Me. These spring from natural tenderness and are worthless if they are not sacrificed or sanctified for Me... sometimes they spring forth because of human compassion... or by sentimentality... caused by the gentle temperament of particular persons; these have no value for heaven.

"Those that the sorrow of contrition bring forth are precious, and I gather them in this chalice. Those that spring forth from humiliation, secretly... from ingratitude suffered in silence... from the effort of self-denial, those My child, quench My thirst, and draw souls near to My Heart.

"The tears of a saintly love, legitimate and resigned, obtain graces.

"Which of these are your tears, child of My Heart? Which are you going to give Me today to dry those that My eyes shed? Do you not wish to drench your own heart with them so as to soften it... melt it... make it worthy of being My comfort, *sacrificing it to Me?*

"I do not want words anymore, My child, but *action* — evident and obvious proof of your progress in virtue... your advances in the denial of worldly things... of the sacrifice of your self-will... of your training in mortification, *through love.* Is not the abundance of the grace that I send from heaven enough to oblige you to strive more and more for perfection? ... Is it too much to ask for fruit from the many graces of favor with which I endow each soul?

"O child, child of My Heart! It is not right

that My eyes shed tears among My children! …
Will you allow My eyes to be blurred by tears
today without drying them with your tenderness and your purpose of amendment?"

Third Meditation

"There are other tears forced by cruel abandonment and distressing desolation… which console My Heart if they are patient.

"There are still others that well up from the
weight of the sins of other people, and those
tightly unite your soul to Me through love.

"Others are very precious and delight Me;
these are the tears that spring from the heart
upon contemplating My Passion, My charity, My
internal sorrow.

"Finally, there are still others that are
squeezed out by gratitude and by the zeal or
longing for the glory of God, which I spilled out
in torrents for the realization of the Redemption,
for the thirst of suffering; and these are priceless, My child, and only in heaven will their
worth be known, and if there were room for
envy, it would be only in order to present Me
with these most precious pearls that the angels
set upon My crown.

"These are the tears that must fill this chalice… those that will quench the thirst of your
Jesus, making Me smile.

"These are the tears that I cannot find in the world… the ones I am looking for… those which must exist among souls that truly love Me… tears of gratitude toward Me, to Whom they owe so much… tears burst forth from the zeal of My Glory… tears because of the souls that are lost… tears of love from a thirst for more suffering just to console Me! Amen."

RESPONSE

O Jesus, Jesus my beloved Jesus! You, crying among Your beloved children? You, not feeling happy in Your Sanctuary? Your eyes dimmed with tears among Your children? O no, never, Jesus of my heart! Here I am to wipe Your tears with my own tears of love and of pain.

I love You, Lord, I love You in the midst of my tears.… I love You in suffering, in a very intimate and unequaled way, in Your very martyrdom.… I love You crucified, and if You would crush me or tear me to pieces, I would love You all the more, Life of my life!

I love You, Jesus, in humiliation and darkness.… I love You in the agony of helplessness.… Lord, if You place me at the bottom of an abyss, I would still love You from that abyss; and if You put me in heaven, I would love You from heaven.… This is how Your children love You.

I love You, I love YOU! Without even pretending that You pay attention to me.... It is an essential need of my life to love You.... You are my breath, Jesus, my respiration, my own heart.

Do not cry any longer, my Dear One, here are my eyes and my whole soul to do it for You.... With Your grace I will fill that golden chalice, and day by day, weeping shall soak my heart for those who offend You... for those who are lost, for the devouring hunger of seeing You loved... for the eagerness of sacrifices, for the delirium of crucifixion and of martyrdom for Your glory.

Holiest Virgin, my beloved Mother, Queen of the Martyrs, crucify my heart together with your own heart at the foot of the Cross, and mix my tears with your own tears. Amen.

16

HOLY HOUR

Time

Spiritual Setting: Let us hear the Lord say to each one of us, "My child, I desire to be the absolute Master of all your things…. Collect yourself, at least during this Holy Hour, inside the wound of My Heart, which is open and expecting you… and there, hidden and silent, drink the charity that is its substance… drink its life."

Petition: We will ask the Lord to grant us the grace of belonging completely to Him, for we are still lacking much to dispossess ourselves of our ego.

Response: To give the Lord all of our time today and always, not robbing Him of even a moment for something that is not Him or for Him.

Lord, here I am: a piece of trash, a wretch, a zero.... What do you want, my Jesus? What can I give You, my Life, if I have already given You everything? My soul? It is all Yours.... My body? I think only of sacrificing it to You.... My heart? O my Jesus, is it not all Yours? ... My senses, my faculties, everything... everything in me, is it not Your own?

Speak, my Love, tell me, what is it that You desire of me?

"I want *your time* for Me, My child, for that is not completely Mine. It is not perfect in all of its parts.... No, not all of your moments are Mine, as I desire them to be.... Your body is here but worldly things and your very self rob Me of your heart and your thoughts. Search within yourself and you will see.... Can you, with your hand upon your heart, tell your Jesus that this is not true?"

Lord, it is true.... Unfortunately my time is not what it should be for You.... But what can I do to please You?

"To have Me always present... and to never lose Me from your sight... and to always act with the purest intention of only being pleasing to Me.

"Time is an ongoing gift... a precious gift that many waste, and I do not want this to happen with My beloved children: I wish that their life, day and night, *be a single act of love, in the midst of any cross.*"

SECOND MEDITATION

O yes, my Lord! From now on my life shall be a *continual act of love in the midst of any cross*, I promise You this, and my Tabor will be Your Calvary…. What does any suffering matter to real love? What, when love's pain is *not suffering enough for the Beloved?*

Yes, I give You my time, Jesus of my soul, be it full of roses or of thorns, and if I would be allowed to choose, I would prefer the latter to crown my heart and my head, in union with You… imitating You, for I love You so.

Receive my hours, my moments, my instants, until my death, until my eternity: those minutes will be Yours and only Yours…. But, O my Lord, many times worldly things make me lose that precious time which belongs to You.

"Nobody, My child, can make you lose it, in your innermost being."

Certainly, my Jesus, but then give me *more light and more love* so that I may have You present in every moment…. Come near to me… make me come nearer to You… so that I may inhale and breathe You in… so as to live from Your heat and from Your life… to unite myself to You… to mend myself through contact with

You.... Ah, Jesus, Jesus of my soul! In this manner my time will be Your time, and Your heartbeats my own heartbeats.

What do You say to me, Jesus of my soul? What do You say to me? Speak to my soul; have pity on me.

Third Meditation

"Yes, My child, this is what I want from you, this is what I have been looking for from you — *interior life*… the life of intimacy with Me; and from this day on, before I am hidden from your sight, I am going to leave you a rule so that you can practice it:

"Live within My Heart, and think… act… sacrifice yourself… and LOVE *as it loves.* This is the perfection of time, that which My children must practice.

"Your sleep time is also Mine, because all of your time must belong to Me… so that your body rests only to be strengthened and to serve Me better, but let your heart remain vigilant, imitating Me…; and how can one keep vigil? Loving, without ceasing to love Me… upon awakening, offer Me your heart, that My sacred name comes from your lips… that your heart repeats it with every throb, and with every breath. All of this will be the fruit of your union with Me, and an evident sign that *all of your time is really Mine.*

"What else is it that I am looking for in this, but *union* with Me, with your Jesus? And if My time upon earth and on the altar was and is only yours, why may I not require that your time be *completely* Mine?"

O Jesus of my life, of my time, of my eternity! You clasp my tenderness tightly with Your kindness and You make my soul burn, under the yoke of Your charms.

My soul is wounded by the arrows of Your glance, of Your humility, of Your unending kindness; my heart is on fire, and I do not *desire*, or *long* for, or *wish* for anything more than Your arms in which to rest. Like a little bird wounded by the hunter, I cannot move from Your side. O Life of my life! You are my existence! You, my dream, my Master, my life's only treasure! My Lord, my soul is all Yours and I wish to saturate You with my tenderness, as You saturate me with Your Cross. O yes, my Jesus! Embody this Cross within my whole being… so that this holy oil may penetrate the deepest parts of my being. I feel such a powerful attraction, such a mighty flight of my spirit toward You, my Eucharistic Jesus, my Jesus Victim, that I wish to do nothing else but to atone for offenses in union with You, wrapping You in an atmosphere of kisses, of sighs, of sacrifices, and of tears.

My Jesus, crush this substance if it is an obstacle to my union with You, and that my soul, *Your soul*, this soul that is completely Yours, may fly up to that atmosphere of infinite fire, to burn, and live eternally inflamed without being consumed, always loving, praising You constantly… satiating itself with You, without ever being satisfied, seeing You at last without veils, contemplating that Ocean of never-before-imagined beauty…. O how I do love You so, so much, my Eucharistic Jesus! But here I only feel You, touch You with my love, with my thoughts, with my faith.

It is true that Your breath touches me during Holy Communion… and I see Your smiles… and Your gaze surrounds me, the thorns of Your forehead touch my own forehead…. I hug You against my heart… and I feel Your fire… and I listen to Your heartbeats, and I count them, and Your beauty dazzles me… and Your Cross makes me fall in love with it…. But in spite of all of this, ah, my Dear One! I feel *empty* and I desire to attach Heart to heart with these same thorns, and to live and to die nailed with the same nails, sacrificed with Your same sacrifices, for only in this way will I be happy.

O Mary! Grant me such great joy; I ask you to say a prayer for me. Amen.

17

HOLY HOUR

Three Doves

Spiritual Setting: We shall see Jesus, showing us His precious wounds which are as radiant as the sun, saying to us, "Do you want to hide yourselves within them? ... Do you want to rest in the Sanctuary with Me? Do you want to lift your flight up to heaven? *Come near to Me... remain recollected... and listen.*"

Petition: With all the fervor of our poor souls, let us ask the Lord for the light to recognize the spiritual state in which we find ourselves.

Response: A strong and saintly recollection of spirit, casting away every voluntary distraction.

"'Come, My child,' I said to you one day, 'Come and take refuge in the crevices of the rock....' I am the true rock; and those cavities, what are they but these that I show you today, saying, *'My hands and feet have been pierced'?* ... O My beloved child, 'Come, come,' I shall repeat to you a thousand times; 'Come and hide deep inside the wounds of your Crucified Jesus, Who today is your Cloister, for your happiness!'

"You were running away, My child, lost in the midst of the world, following your own whims... surrounded by snares and dangers... weak and not offering any resistance to the enemy.... Would that you had just been *weak! ...* But even more, you were *imprudent*! Do you remember? You loved danger and you were nearly at the point of perishing... and besides being weak and imprudent, *you were also guilty,* tarnishing your heart, O so many times!

"How very unfortunate you were! You were looking for peace where you could never find it..., you loved what you were supposed to hate..., and you let yourself go into the snare like a little bird, without realizing that there lay a mortal danger for your soul.

"Like a wounded dove you were able to fly astray, poor soul! But you did not know how to come back to Me; you knew how to lose yourself, but not how to save yourself! You could not look up to heaven because you were guilty… you could not look upon the earth because you were disgraced upon it… you wanted to flee, but to where? In anguish you wanted to hide yourself, and *without ever thinking about the only friend of your soul.* One day, He felt sorry for you, and approaching your ear said, 'Come, My dove, and find refuge within the precious wounds you yourself opened with your sins.… Hide yourself within these divine cavities, so sweet because of their love, so fresh with the redeeming blood.… From now on, what can you fear, since you have found your refuge there? … If a hurricane is unleashed, you will not fear the storm.… If the enemy pursues you, you have nothing to fear, hidden in the depths of the rock… within the depth of this holy retreat you will be cured and become happy.' Did you listen to Me?"

Second Meditation

O Jesus of all my soul! How can I repay You for such a great favor? Yes, I heard Your voice and for a long time I hid within Your blessed wounds, and what a great delight it was for me to be submerged in them! Humbled, repentant, and bathed in Your Passion, I returned one day to hear Your voice saying to me, "*Now rise higher, and as a dove that builds its nest in the borders of the highest crevices....* Abandon the low places of the earth.... 'Let the dead bury their dead,' and rise, rise unto the sublime regions of the tabernacle."

And this is what I have come to do, my Jesus, to fix my nest *very far from the earth.* Before I used to find refuge within Your precious wounds with a deep feeling of fear, and now I will settle my nest with much more trust and love. Before I used to hide myself, trembling... but now I will rest peacefully upon the top of this rock and in the sunlight.... Both now and then, I had leaned on the rock, but before, it was as in a temporal shelter to regain my strength, and now it is settling my abode forever inside of this dear tabernacle.... Before, I was wounded and unhappy, I yearned only for the crevice in the rock, but now, upon hearing Your voice calling me, I felt strengthened, my Jesus. I felt wings, and here I am; my soul flutters around the altar and desires to make its nest in the Eucharist. O yes! The Eucharist is this rock which is You, my Jesus; it is the summit of Your love and of Your graces, the summit of my happiness, and it is there where I want to live, and there where I want to die, far away from the world and from my very self. Will You grant me this, my beloved Jesus?

The Eucharist is my life, my center, my strength, my happiness on earth. There, the constant victim of love and sorrow is always present; that Heart of fire inflames and consumes me, there is the nest for a lover of Jesus. But does this flight of the dove, of the enamored soul, end there? O no!

Third Meditation

"Had I but wings like a dove, I would fly away and be at rest," the psalmist king says.

This dove no longer asks for refuge, not even for a nest; it spreads its wings, flies and arrives at a refuge that is no longer of this world: on the summit of the rock it undoubtedly found the nest it needed; but there it was still upon earth... in the same manner that man is made for work, the soul is made for flying.

Very soon this soul, this dove, experiences a strong desire to own the heavens... to be engulfed in the Divinity... to submerge itself in its God... to thrust itself into the infinite and be at last united with its Beloved forever... in the nest of the Eucharist, where it had settled, its strength has increased... its wings have grown and it spreads them and flies, flies in the vast depths of the Divinity, without being able to ever embrace it completely.

O my God! And when will this soul thrust itself to rest in Your bosom? Happy flight... blessed repose.

Ah! Undoubtedly the Eucharist is worth more than everything there is upon earth… more than all the riches… more than all the honors… even more than all the graces that we receive from God upon the earth.… But the Eucharist is not heaven in the sense that Jesus is hidden, covered by the Eucharistic veils — and heaven shows Him to us *uncovered*.… The Eucharist requires faith and love, and heaven asks only for love.

And so, Lord, Lord, who will give us those wings to fly to heaven and rest there? When, my God, when will we be untied from this mortal flesh? When will the ego not prevent us from flying toward You, Jesus of my soul? When will we have our delight in the midst of internal reflection … in the emptiness of worldly things … in the silence of our hearts? When will we find peace and joy in the Cross, even when we are nailed to it?

O, Love of all loves! Sustain my poor soul which thrusts itself so high without being worthy of it! Crucify it, turn it to dust, humble it, for it is only through humility that one can ascend… and the loftiest flight must begin within the most profound depths. Burn my imperfections with the fire of Your love… lighten the weight of my self-love and pride… give me, my Eucharistic Jesus, constancy to persevere… fortitude to suffer… a hunger for sacrifice and an unquenchable thirst for You, because my soul experiences within itself the cruel martyrdom of still being far away from You.

RESPONSE

O God of my life, Jesus of my soul, adorable Word! These are the steps of the ascent that my soul desires to follow in order to reach You: Your divine wounds… the Eucharist… heaven… if I am persecuted by the enemy, Your wound! … If I want to delight in Your peace, the Eucharist; if I die, heaven.

O Jesus, my Jesus, my enchanting Jesus enclosed in this consecrated Host! I ask only three things of You, and tell me today, before this Blessed Hour is over, these moments of heaven I spend near to You, that You are going to grant them to me: a *refuge* in Your wounds as a dove… a *nest* like the dove near to You, very near to You inside Your Heart, in the tabernacle… and finally, a *repose* for the dove in heaven, in the arms of the Word, under the most tender gaze of the Father, wrapped by the infinite love of the Holy Spirit at Mary's side. Amen.

18

HOLY HOUR

If Only You Knew…

Spiritual Setting: Let us contemplate Jesus, as divine as always, but with a sad face and deep feeling, as He says to each of us: *"O My child, if only you knew the gift of God!"*

Petition: Today let us ask the Lord to know that gift and to love it and be grateful for it with all our soul, brushing away the sadness from His Heart.

Response: This week we shall make constant acts of reparation for our lack of responses — so many of them! — that have until now filled our prayer life.

"Here we are once again alone for an hour, My child… away from the world and its distractions… and intimately united Heart to heart, and you are going to listen to My complaints.

"If only you knew the gift of God! If you could understand the ardent interest your soul inspires in Me! … If you could realize the real pleasures hidden in sacrifice, in that life of self-denial, in that life of voluntary and constant crucifixion which you ought to practice and that you do not!

"If you would appreciate this pearl of *love for the Cross* which I have given you… a sublime love studded with many special graces! Ah, My child, how very differently you would act!

"If only you knew, I repeat, the gift of God, how differently you would live! … How your tepidity would be changed into fire! How your weak spirit of self-denial would be changed into generosity toward Me! How your wantonness would be changed into recollection! How those thoughts that detain you with worldly things would be for Me! How your lack of faith would be illuminated by My brightness. How your in-action, My dear child, would fly to action with a fervent love for sacrifice!

"And why is it not that way? Why is it that I find filth where everything should be clean? Why does the iciness — of self-love that freezes everything, of that self-indulgence that darkens your spirit, of that meager love for penitence that makes your soul ugly — touch your heart?

"If only you knew the gift of God, you would not do all of this. Rather, clean and pure of all blemishes, humbled and generous, you would fly through the ways of perfection without a rest, without a stop, impelled by love, sacrificing yourself every moment without any self-interest, and only to please Me."

SECOND MEDITATION

Jesus is sad and afflicted: He desires more love, more self-denial... more perfection from His children.... *"More, More!"* is the cry that is heard from the tabernacle. Poor Jesus!

Weary, as He seated Himself at Jacob's well in that Blessed Hour when He was saving a soul — let us contemplate Him today with that inspired hue, with those loving gazes, with that enchanting attitude as He also says to us, "He Who is speaking to you *is your God.* Do not hesitate; *this is the right time, this is the time of your salvation... learn to recognize the gift of God!"*

O my Jesus! If only I would have been able to seize at least a spark escaping from Your eyes at that moment... if I had been able to hear that fatigued breath, that unforgettable, inimitable and irresistible tone with which You must have pronounced these words: *"If only you knew the gift of God, you would love Him, and if you loved Him, you would be saved."*

Well, this Jesus Whom we now have before our eyes… is the same Savior Who complains… Who asks for the water of virtue… and Who offers us that other water, as He did to the Samaritan woman, the water which would quench our thirst forever.

O Jesus of all my soul! You also tired Yourself over me, a miserable sinner, looking for me in the midst of so many dangers, vanities, and excesses. You became tired from looking for me and bringing me back to Yourself… so many times and in so many ways, You called me with these words that made my heart quake: "If only you knew the gift of God," and I — so ungrateful! — how many times did I not wish to hear You and made myself deaf to Your goodness?

But, Lord, at last I am here, beside You, in Your Heart. O, and how blessed I am! And what is it that You want me to do? That "gift of God" that today in loving complaint You make to me — is it the gift of my love for the Cross to which I have so poorly responded and so little appreciated — is this the gift of which You are speaking? Tell me, Lord, I beg you, is this the one You are speaking about? What is it that I should know, and which is the gift to which I do not respond enough?

"This gift, My child, is that of peace bound in sacrifice… in the Cross that is embraced for love of Me, never letting go of it. That peace that the world does not know and never finds amidst pleasures, comfort, incense, and self-satisfaction.… This gift is certainly your love for My Cross, for that Cross which gushes with caresses… for that Cross of which its riches you shall never tire of counting… for the Cross that carries My Heart as the center of its charity in order to cast its fire over the world and its charity to millions of souls.… That gift is the one that here, at the foot of the altar, you will swallow in great gulps, sweetening with it all of your sorrows.… O, I will repeat it to you a thousand times, child of My soul: If only you knew the gift that God has given you by bringing you to know the riches of suffering, and making you fall in love with suffering to the point of delirium; to inebriate yourself with its sweetness… to discover its charms… to triumph over yourself… to transform yourself in Me through love.

"This precious gift, My child, is the forgiveness of all your sins, and your failures… ingratitude, and infidelities — so numerous — because the Cross erases everything… in the Cross there is salvation; in the Cross, life, mercy, and tenderness. There, Justice was satisfied, and with that Cross, that blood-stained key, I opened heaven for you.

"This gift is also the support of your weakness, your fortitude and shield against temptations and even from all hell itself.... This gift is ultimately Myself, your Jesus; the same Jesus of the Samaritan woman, weary from reaching out to you, tired and worn out by your ingratitude, by your lack of response, by the delays you always give Me on your way to perfection.

"I was pouring more and more graces upon you, and you were wasting them! I was enveloping you with My special favors, and you were only getting used to them and not thinking about their worth or being grateful for them! Your rashness, your weakness... your inner wantonness... your routine in My service... your weak spirit of faith. O My beloved child! All of this renders you to have very little generosity towards Him Who died for you.

"Have you now known the gift of God? All of what I have said is this gift, summarized, stated perfectly upon the Cross; but how could I make you savor the Cross in the manner I know is pleasing to you, so that you do not reject it? How can I make you embrace it, if you repel it? ... How can I put it before you so that you do not resist it?

"If you would finally renounce yourself... if you would be firm and constant in your resolutions... if worldly things and events would not sway you... IF YOU COULD ONLY SAVOR

THE CROSS… if you would really love Me to the point of sacrifice… if you would really love Me, O child of the Cross! Then… then you would know the gift of God, and I would drown you in infinite delight in this life, and be your recompense through all eternity."

RESPONSE

My Jesus, beloved Master of my soul! What can I say but that You are right, Lord; that my ungrateful behavior towards You contradicts my vocation… that You cry while I laugh… that You reach out Your arms toward me, and that I turn my back to You… that I have not known or appreciated the gift of God nor have I been grateful for it — ah! How I have deserved to have it taken away from me because of my lack of sensitivity toward You, because my promises have been wanting, and my offerings so vain that they evaporate upon appearing?

O Jesus of my soul! In this miserable state, will I continue to live my life, which should be a life of active, generous and very loving sacrifice? No, my Jesus, from now on I promise to be a true repose for Your Heart, a true child, knowing and loving the gift of God with all my strength.

Mary, celestial Mother of my soul, make me know, love, and give thanks for the gift of God. Amen.

19

HOLY HOUR

Cloister of the Heart

Spiritual Setting: Today we shall see Jesus present and real upon the altar. Fixing a glance full of tenderness upon us, and with His arms outstretched in the form of the Cross, He says to each one of us, "Do you want Me to be your Cloister? Do you wish to live within Me? Fly, My dear soul, fly today and enter the wound in My side, as a dove into its nest."

Petition: With all the fervor of our hearts, we shall ask to never leave the interior of Jesus.

Response: Let us remember throughout the day that we must live inside of Him… with His same blood… with His same heartbeats, keeping the internal concentration that the presence of God requires.

"See, My child, earthly cloisters enclose bodies, but many souls do not live therein.... Jesus, your Refuge, Who is the true Cloister, will enclose both the bodies and the souls of those who give themselves truly up to Me.

"This is why I wish to enclose you within Myself, inside a Lily — but a blood-stained Lily... inside a fragrant Lily which perfumes everything it touches with its purity.

"And that Lily... that Easter Lily, Who can it be but your Jesus in the form of a Cross, taking the harshness from your suffering, and the bitterness from your pain? Will you then enclose yourself forever inside of this white Cloister, in the form of the Cross?

"This is the true enclosed garden... this is the true enclosure, divine and silent, for those who love Me... here is where internal solitude and contemplation are learned.

"But I have terms to set; do not be upset, My child, for I will multiply the reward for your efforts.

"I require that you die to yourself, so as to resurrect in Me.

"I asked you for your body, do you remember? And you gave it to Me dead to yourself, with the determination of giving your body no pleasure... of not following its whims... of not pampering it, etc. It must be like a corpse for everyone else, despicable and loathsome… and then it shall all the more be Mine… and if your soul is clean and pure, your Jesus will cherish it.

"One can enter into this true Cloister — which I, Jesus, am — only when one is dead to every self-love. O child of My soul, give Me all of your affections; hand them over to Me, and I will polish them much better than you could.… I promise you to do so… your affections shall be *ever more Mine* according to the generosity of your sacrifice. I will purify them within My Heart. Will you give them to Me today, or will you deny them to Me Who, stretching out My arms toward you, is asking for them?

"Contemplate My tears and do not deny your Jesus your affections."

Second Meditation

O Jesus of all my soul, of my life, of all my being! You, crying? … Asking me for a sacrifice that You will repay with heaven? Could I refuse? Impossible! Even if there were no heaven, I would love You… even if You gave me no reward — is not the greatest joy to sacrifice myself for You? Is not the greatest of love's sufferings that of not suffering enough for the Beloved?

With what merits do I wish to acquire the

title that even the angels would envy, namely that of BEING YOUR CROSS, of bearing that name on my body and in my soul — of being a child of Your Heart?

What would it matter that my heart bleeds, if it is You, my Jesus, who melts me with Your glance, who asks me this to console Your Heart?

Why should I want worldly things if I have YOU? My Jesus, who but I is honored with what You propose to me?

To live inside of You! For You to be my Cloister, my own life! O heavenly secret! I shall be all Yours, love of my heart and of my whole being, and I shall happily go through everything You wish! I renounce my own will and everything that I can, to heal the entrance to Your Heart that widens itself to receive me! O happiness!

Do You accept me, even though I am not worthy? ... Do You enclose me inside this Immaculate Lily so as to receive its purity, its fragrance and its whiteness?

Answer me, my Jesus, for I am dying to hear You.... I feel Your warmth embrace me, I feel Your grandeur surround me.... Stop, Jesus. Do not come near to me, because You will stain Yourself — but then how can I enter into that wound that is my heaven? ... Even if I cannot have a religious vocation, I can still be Yours anywhere that Your Will places me.

"O, My child! You can be My spouse, with the veil of purity, with the clothing of sacrifice, and by renouncing everything that is not Me.

"I love you so... and you have wounded My Heart.

"Those sighs which you have hidden, in the desire of being all Mine... those tears that welled up from the bottom of your heart, silently, for a dreamt Beloved... that martyrdom which filled your heart with the desire of belonging completely to Me... this, child, attracted Me to you and drew grace upon grace from Me.

"And today all of this is no longer an illusion; you have touched reality by your complete surrender to My Will.

"Have you not experienced yourself free and without ties, very near to Me? ... Have you not trembled with joy seeing the culmination of your hopes? ... I am all yours... I will be the Spouse of your soul... My ears shall hear the words of your mouth; your sighs shall be all Mine."

O Jesus, my Jesus, do not say anything more; I love You, I love You... do not let Your tenderness melt me.

"Ask, ask whatever you wish, because today I cannot deny you anything.... It is Love's Day."

Jesus, You ask first! For I can deny You nothing....

"I desire that you model your life according to My life... living inside of Me."

Yes, Jesus I promise You this! ... And what shall I ask? ... I ask You for the salvation of souls... I ask to always do Your will.

"See, I open My arms, My Heart, and My side to you.... Here you will find unbreakable bars that will guard you from all your enemies.... Mary will be your director, and you will bind yourself to give her an account of your conscience every day, every hour or whenever you desire to do so. She will guide you inside of your Cloister — Jesus.... She will teach you to immerse yourself in My life... in My Passion... in My virtues.... Throw yourself into her arms for she will be your teacher... your comfort... your treasure.... She is the only one to completely know the interior of your Jesus. She will now bring forth the roses, then the thorns upon your brow and in your heart... and you shall be her child, and thus, *completely and forever Mine.*"

RESPONSE

O Jesus, Jesus of my soul! What can I say overwhelmed as I am by Your favors? My Lord, all words are too mute and cold to express the gratitude of my heart.

The world cannot understand the incomparable happiness that inundates me; those the world embraces are only shadows.

I would like everyone to know my happiness is a thousandfold because I am Yours! I would like to cry out, to shout that my joy in my *Cloister Jesus* is a thousandfold! I wish that everything in heaven and upon earth would join me in praising the absolute Master of my whole being.

My Jesus... my Love... my Life... my Cloister! I am willing to sacrifice myself together with You, my crucified Spouse... no more resistance... I am going to enter a new spiritual stage and I ask You for Your grace, Your strength, Your protection. You know how very miserable I am, but let come whatever You Will; *I am Yours*... from this moment I throw myself into Your depth, like a dove to its nest... and there cut... pluck... and crucify me... Your Will shall be my own. If I were annihilated, if I were cut into pieces, I would still not be able to repay the grace You have granted me today.

Mary, Mary, have pity on your child who loves you so! Amen.

20

HOLY HOUR

Love
(Holy Thursday)

Spiritual Setting: Today, recalling the institution of the Sacrament of our Love, we shall contemplate Jesus ardent and illuminated, revealing the warmth of His tenderness. Thus we shall see Him approach us and invite us to rest our tired heads upon His shoulder.... His holy mouth remains close to our ear, and ours — O my God! — ours is upon His fiery Heart.

Petition: Today, we shall ask for the grace of not being able to live without the Eucharist for even a moment.

Response: *To burn... to consume ourselves... to give ourselves completely and forever to the Eucharistic Jesus, without ever returning to take ourselves back,* living from His life as victim and abandoning ourselves to His Will.

Today I can only meditate upon love, and only on the love of the Eucharist. Those words: "Take and eat... this is My Body; take and drink... this is My Blood," and I can do nothing other than to take and *eat*... to take and *drink*... satisfying my soul with the insatiable.

O Charity that inflames my heart and consumes it without consuming it! My heart, my soul, and even my body, with all of its beats and feelings, cannot separate itself — O no — from that Immaculate Host, because it is my heaven, because it exerts upon them the indescribable attraction of Divinity!

Behind the thin veil with which the Incarnate Word covers Himself, my heart perceives Him... feels Him... touches Him... contemplates Him... caresses Him, and loves Him, and is unfortunate only because it is not able to wring out all of its blood to defend the truth of this Mystery.

O my Eucharistic Jesus! Why do You not make me a martyr of Your love? O White Host of my life Who is purity itself! Why do You not whiten my blackness? Why do You not also transform me into a host, into a victim?

I would like to be Your altar, Jesus of the Tabernacle... Your ciborium... Your pyx... the very obscurity that envelops You!

I cannot find the way to be ever closer to You, ever more united to Your substance! I would like to be Your image of constant sacrifice … I, Your image, to duplicate You, being only one, to give You more… to be more crucified.

Host of my life, I wish to have Your ability to not let a moment go by without sacrificing myself for souls.… Will You grant me this today?

Second Meditation

"My child, you shall be altar, priest, and victim.… You will sacrifice yourself every day on behalf of the Church, even though you are not worthy. Victim souls, united to the Eucharistic Host, have a special title in My Heart… and My court will be formed by those pure and sacrificed *generous souls* who will be ever more Mine, offering themselves up for the sake of others.

"I desire victim souls so as to obtain My purposes.… I desire pure souls for the salvation of the world.… The Cross is the shield of My chosen souls and of My Church, and the triumph of the Eucharist in souls.

"Do you love the Eucharist, as you are telling Me? Well, then, *crucify yourself for its honor*, loving the Cross."

O Jesus of my soul! I love and adore the Eucharist and I will be a martyr in its honor. I wish to be a living cross and a reflection of You, crucified. My soul, upon contemplating the Cross and the Tabernacle, takes up such a flight that it ascends, and rises overcoming my rubbish, desiring to embrace, to unite itself, lose itself, and incorporate itself into that consecrated Host. Do You know why, my Lord? It is because of the hunger of self-effacement, of silence, of fire, and of *suffering*, which devours me.

But what kind of grace is this, my Jesus? It is only natural in a child of the Crucified… in a soul enamored of the Cross, in a child of Your love.

These aspirations seem to be arrogant, but no, Lord, they are cries, expressions of love, which You communicate from the Tabernacle.

How would it be possible today, here, drinking from the fountain of Your Heart of fire, for my soul not to burn, imitating You in always being pure, and always being a victim?

THIRD MEDITATION

O Lord, the more that I touch the abyss of my misery… and the more that it imprisons My heart, this spirit breaks the bonds with which I press it against the earth of my nothingness, and it escapes from me and is propelled toward that divine throne which encloses its life, its center, its happiness, its Word.

What do I do, what must I do if it does not desire to quiet itself in the ponds which encircle it, but is looking for the bottomless, shoreless sea of its Eucharist? I plunge this spirit into the narrow pit of self-knowledge; but in this plunging it acquires strength and takes flight and is propelled to that immensity of its God, the only one that is able to satisfy it.

O why — so tiny and poor — does my heart have those flights, that thirst, that suffocation, shall I say, in everything that is not great, that is to say, in everything that is not God?

If I am not able to embrace a drop of suffering, why do I long to contain a sea? If I am only a small point in space, why do I desire to possess that infinite and thrice Holy Judge in my heart?

I know what happens, Lord: it is that the drop is lost in the midst of the sea, and nothingness is lost in infinity... it is because my soul *"shares in the Master's joys"* when it receives the Holy Eucharist.... It is because He absorbs me and carries me into His immensity.

O Eucharist of my life, infinity in one location! With what speed my soul runs the distances to You, and sees and understands without understanding, neither seeing nor knowing what You are... absorbed in a single point, but an infinite point… a point of uncreated love, where one breathes life, satisfaction, and endless joy, without measure of time.

O adorable Eucharist! You are the center of my ardent desires and celestial love! If I could have the language of the Seraphim, I would employ it only in praising You! If we could only understand *what* Jesus in the Eucharist is for us! His charms enthrall me… His attraction draws me… His perfections absorb me… His light attracts me… His fire burns me!

My life is fused there, in that sacred Urn, in that immaculate Host. There my Treasure, my Master, my Divine Word, my Beloved, is found. O that all my heartbeats could be Communions! O that all the moments of my life could be just for Him! I am scorched, I burn because I am under the same roof, breathing the same air that Jesus breathes… feeling myself bathed in His glance… when I come, electrified, to adore Him. Being with Him fills all the needs of my life.

Without Him, O my God, I would not live! It would be impossible for me to exist! O whitest Host of my life! My eyes rest upon You with tenderness… in You my heart finds strength; my imperfections are consumed with every step in that volcano of love.

O Jesus! O Ciborium of my life! O Lily of the Tabernacle! O Divine Sun of my love! Please bless us today and grant us the grace to be assimilated to You in purity and in sacrifice.

Mary, first Tabernacle where Jesus dwelt, give us your love so as to know how to love Him with perfection. Amen.

21

HOLY HOUR

He Is All Mine... I Am All His

Spiritual Setting: Today we shall contemplate the risen Lord Who, full of glory, says to each one of us: "If you are all Mine, I shall be all yours."

Petition: Lord, grant us the grace to be only Yours, to expel our ego from our soul far away from ourselves, and to trample on it, for it decreases Your possession of our being.

Response: During this entire week, let us savor these very sweet and delectable words, not permitting their perfume be snatched away by distraction: "He is all mine... I am all His."

"My child, at your every instant and breath, I desire that you always say that *you are all Mine:* This is the music of love that makes Me forget many ingratitudes. This tune is so sweet to My ears! But, whenever your lips tell Me that you are all Mine, if your heart does not say so with actions of self-abandonment, of annihilation of the self, and of mortification, you will not be so; you will be very far from belonging to Me.

"You see, when worldly things occupy your thoughts YOU ARE NOT MINE.... When you occupy your memory and your will, you are not all Mine.... When your heart is not void of earthly affections, you are not all Mine.... When your self-love and your self-judgment intervene with obedience and mortification... you are not all Mine.

"It is certainly true that you were born to renounce yourself... to cease existing for yourself, *and to give yourself to others*; but you cannot attain this goal if you do not first belong completely to Me, renouncing yourself and molding yourself with your Crucified Jesus, Who loves you so.

"In what do you now resemble your Jesus? Examine yourself, My child, here in My presence, slowly; set your hand upon your heart and tell Me, here in this silence which surrounds us...

in this blessed hour that My kindness grants you… in this place chosen for My tabernacle, and where the lilies form crosses, and the crosses, lilies… in what do you resemble your Beloved? Do you always have a tendency to mortification and humility? … Does the thirst for sacrifice consume you? Do you always long to withdraw from the affection of worldly things and from yourself, so that I may appear? Do you think about yourself, and not only about Me?

"In an intimate and hidden life, My love is satisfied. And yours?

"O My child, My child! When I desired to create a place for the angels, I spread the vault of the firmament under them… and when I wished to create a space for Myself, I formed your heart…. With what are you going to respond to so great a love?"

SECOND MEDITATION

"In this way, My child, you will be all Mine: imitate Me in your heart with these virtues; but today I am going to give you a *secret*, and if you practice it, it will, in a short time, throw you into My arms. Do you know what it is? 'TO ALWAYS CHOOSE TO SUFFER.' This is sublime… this is more than to always do what is more perfect, and if you put yourself to work on this you shall realize what the difference is in this matter.

"This exercise will lead you to be more united to Me Who *always chose to suffer for you….* Imitate Me, child; you yourself must take the axe in your hand and cut yourself into splinters, shattering your self-will… wounding your heart… wrecking your ego. Will you deny Me this? Could this be possible, child of My soul?

"After having been the chosen one from among many thousands… the favorite of My tenderness…, will you stop… will you hesitate when suffering comes, as you contemplate your crucified Master?

"O no, you shall be Mine, all Mine, forever Mine, and the world will not steal from Me this which has cost Me so much, a child of My love… a lily for My garden… a spouse for My Heart.

"Certainly, your wings are still short, but do not fear; they shall grow if you are faithful, and you will fly, you will fly inside of My Heart which is your Cloister, and you shall know the secrets that are still hidden to your eyes now.

"Tell Me: our time is almost finished and I desire to hear that delightful music… *tell Me that you love Me…* tell Me that you are and always will be Mine, and that you belong only to your Jesus.

"Look, My child: all of creation is nothing to Me, compared with a single act of love from the heart of man… and I am happy only *where I receive love.* This is all I ask from every soul: love... love... love, which is born, remains and grows only under the heat of suffering... of self-renunciation... of voluntary crucifixion.

"Choose, then, child of My soul, to always suffer... and then, then you will be truly Mine and I will possess you and you will possess Me, absorbing you... making you divine... and Myself also becoming yours, totally yours."

THIRD MEDITATION

"When your soul is *completely pure*, I will be all yours, as far as your weakness can contain Me. And what is it to be *all yours?* To absorb you, My child, I repeat, to transform you into Myself, to form one heart with yours, and to be, O yes! the center of all your aspirations.

"To be *all yours* is to unite Myself to you with an indissoluble unity of love and suffering.... It is to have the very same life, a single will, the same Cross.... Can there be a greater happiness?

"The soul that does not take itself into consideration for anything, that annihilates itself, that discounts and dismisses itself, and that gives itself up to the Cross with complete detachment and without reservation, will come to possess Me, and in the height of its venture, will enthusiastically exclaim: 'No longer I, but Jesus in me…. He, all mine, and I all His!'

"Can there be a greater happiness upon earth and in heaven?

"A God, yours? … Yes, child of My soul, A GOD, YOURS… a Eucharistic Jesus, Who day and night sacrifices Himself for you… Who always longs to come down in Communion, for this is the end where His humility stops and in which His love is satisfied because, child, I, your Jesus, even though I am God, cannot be all yours in Communion if I do not sacrifice Myself beforehand. And you, will you by chance *desire and be able to be all Mine* if you do not die to yourself and sacrifice yourself, and let yourself be sacrificed also?

"Cheer up, then, and be brave, My child! For the only sorrow for hearts, their only torment, must be not suffering enough for the Beloved. A beautiful ideal, and happy the soul that accomplishes this refinement of love."

RESPONSE

Yes, Life of my life! *I, all Yours… and You, all mine.* This will be the sole aspiration of my life: to belong to You and that You belong to me… to love the Cross ardently, and to be a victim in union with You, nailing myself upon it! There, there

You shall be *more mine*, in the same measure of my voluntary sacrifice: my heaven upon earth will be to mold myself with the Crucified of my soul. Even in my lowliness I experience the passion, the attraction of a *love of immolation.* I feel anxious for perfection with an unknown stress.... I want to embrace all the virtues, my Jesus. To suffer and to love, to love and to suffer, and life seems too short for me so as to be a holocaust for my Beloved!

O Lord of my soul! And who could never have offended You! O Heart of my soul! Who could always have loved You! Jesus, Jesus! From now on, my heart will not beat except to give You glory, to humble itself, to suffer and to be forever Yours!

I wish to be a fire to melt the icy mountains that exist in human hearts and to warm Jesus Who experiences cold, even in the souls of those who call themselves His own.

I wish to be all balm to soothe Your wounds.... I am already, in my happiness, and through a very special grace, Your child, and I shall be fortunate and happy, plucking all the thorns from Your Heart one by one, being all Yours... and You all mine, Jesus of my soul, *all, all and forever mine!*

Give Him to me, Mary; put Him into my arms and into my poor heart. Amen.

22

HOLY HOUR

I Am at the Door

Spiritual Setting: Today we will see Jesus, Who is looking into the pupils of our eyes with an intimate love, touching the door of our heart with His divine hand.

Petition: Today we shall ask the all-good Jesus that we not turn deaf ears to His calling, but that we promptly respond to His inspiration.

Response: All during this week we will keep a profound seclusion so as to hear the sweet sound of His voice in the depths of our souls.

FIRST MEDITATION
"I am at the door and I am knocking."

What is this I hear! … Is it You, my Jesus, Who directs these words to me, the One Who is so near to me — my God! — the One Who, without getting tired, waits like a beggar at the threshold of my heart?

"It is I, My child, I Who am always looking for you… Who constantly calls you with solicitude.… I am your Jesus, Who watches while you sleep… Who cries when you stray… Who looks for you while you think only about worldly things or of yourself… Who in a thousand ways and by infinite means knocks at the door of your ungrateful and frozen heart."

To penetrate the heart of man is the *only ambition of God.*… Everything in heaven and on the earth belongs to Him… and — alas! — only the human heart has the sad power to remove Him from His empire.… This heart that Jesus is asking of us is the profound refuge in which the fragile majesty of our being is hidden.… If our heart is free, we are free… if it is obedient, we are submissive… if it is in the world, even though we might be religiously oriented, we would be worldly… and if it is in God, we are God's. But the heart *is freely surrendered;* it is not forced: even divine power stops before this impenetrable threshold. God, Who has given us our heart, Himself respects it, and prefers to bow down before this dignity, leaving it completely to us, so as to diminish it, overwhelm it.... This is why He says, *"Child, give Me your heart,"* and for this *He is at the door, and He is knocking.*

"Ever since the day you were born, My child, I am at your door, desiring your whole heart; but... has it been Mine? ... How many times have you harshly closed the door in My Face, preferring the world... the vanities... the occupations... worldly creatures... even Satan disguised? ... Look back and tell Me, if you can, that it has not been so.

"How many knocks did your conversion cost Me? ... How many delays did you give Me? ... How many times, my dear soul, did you laugh, and I was lamenting this with sighs and tears right next to you.... You resisted Me with haughtiness, and I insisted *humbly* with incomparable motivation.... And when once You did come to open your heart, did you not experience My enthusiasm and rejoicing?

"And today, what can you say? ... Have I never cried at the door of your heart? ... Have I not had to await *humbly* — and with the patience of God, and with pearls in My hands... and amidst the noise of your pride — for you to hear Me.... What have I done for you except benefit you? ... What am I asking for except that which should be Mine, that is, your *heart* — but a clean… pure… open… loving… generous… and sacrificed heart? Is this how you give it to Me?"

Second Meditation

Lord of my soul! I have been ungrateful, even more than ungrateful, to You… and I cannot bear Your humiliation without asking You for pardon, my Jesus, without crying because of my infidelities, without offering amendment.

Today, Jesus, it is my turn. O yes! Changing our roles, Lord, kneeling, humble and contrite, here I am at the doors of Your Heart and I am knocking.… If I have been deaf… if I have been a *sinner*, if I have been proud, harsh, miserable, and ungrateful, You are not like that.… Listen to me and open… open that Heart of fire, so as to consume all my failures in it.… The language of my spirit will be that of humility and prayer, that always find an echo in Your soul.

Your kindness, Jesus, will not allow me to forget my *poverty* and my *nothingness*… and I promise You to be at the disposal of Your Will and of Your love.

I place myself at the feet of Him Who is my Life and my Treasure.… If You, my Beloved, are willing to rush to bring happiness to my heart, I will enthusiastically tell You a thousand times, "Lord I am not worthy to receive You in my poor dwelling; it is up to me to come to the doors of Your Heart, and I shall be healed." ... I am not worthy to occupy the place that You have prepared for me in Your Heart. And what can I say? The words of the sinful woman: *"Lord, have pity on me, I am a great sinner."*

My humility and my prayer, I repeat, will make You surrender, my beloved, dear Jesus, to pardon me. You have said, *"Ask and it will be given to you,"* and as if You had not completed Your thought, *"Seek and you shall find";* and, as if this were not yet enough, Lord of my soul, You added, *"Knock... knock, and it will be opened for you."* Well, then, with this celestial security, with an unlimited confidence, born out of love, today I knock on the door of Your Heart, with my sighs, with my pleading... with my promises and with my tears. Will You open it for me, adorable Jesus? I will nevermore be unfaithful.... Look, I will live the life of a voluntary victim abandoned to Your Will, in expiation for so many hearts, like my own heart, who have not been willing to hear that *You are knocking....* I will be pure and saintly.... I will sing a canticle of love in the midst of my suffering... I will suffer in silence and will fight bravely against everything that seems to move me away from You.... Are You moved, Heart of Jesus? Do You hear that I am at Your door and I am knocking?

"Yes, I hear you, My dear child, child of My Heart.... If you knock with the Cross, how could I not open the dwelling place that My love has prepared for you, if this is where your asylum is, your place, your nest?

"But, look: in this third meditation neither you nor I will knock on our hearts... neither you nor I will knock so that it will open for us. The sublime moment of the mystical union has arrived and the flame of our most pure and saintly love has broken open and invites us to an eternal embrace.

"Do you not see that I have said to you: *'Come to Me, all you who labor and are burdened, and I will give you rest'?* ... Have I not come down to the earth, have I not remained under these species of the Sacrament to be nearer to you? ... Do I not live with you; do you not live with Me, and for what, My dear child? Is it not to be able to communicate our mutual affection and the saintly confidences of our souls without witnesses?

"But there still remains a small distance between both of us, *and you know what this is....* Conquer it... with humility, yes, but with ardor and confidence, so that I might rest upon you without being hurt, repose in you... spill out My treasures upon your soul... give you My love completely, having you enjoy the incomparable pleasures enclosed in *your precious vocation to suffering."*

Lord of my soul, Master of my life! Knock upon my heart… I will knock on Yours… let neither of us knock… whatever You desire, my Beloved, whatever You wish: just to not be unfaithful to You is my frenzy; just to dry Your tears, my ambition… just to cure Your wounds, my occupation… just to form a place of rest for You, the only ambition of my life. That our hearts may never again be closed to each other — mine through my ingratitude, and Yours because of my ingratitude — O no! My good Jesus, my beloved Jesus, my charming Jesus! No more resistance to Your inspirations…. Alas! No more keeping You waiting at the door of my soul as I did so many other times… no more making You sad and causing Your tears… You, crying, here, in this place where You should only smile? Never again!

With the purity of my behavior, with the constant sacrifice of my will, and with the saintly ardor of my love, I will prepare the atmosphere around Your tabernacle for You to inhale: I will adorn Your altar with the flowers of virtues, watered with repentance.... This love in which I am consumed will open the little door of the tabernacle, as well as that of Your Heart, and there, I will set my nest... and here, You will place Your own... O my Jesus, humiliated by me so many times, like a beggar! *No more,* Lord; and from now on everything will be for Your sake... self-denial, generosity, response, and love!

Holy Virgin, who like no one else was faithful in the loving response to grace, grant that the door of my heart be always open for your Jesus! Amen.

23

HOLY HOUR

My Ideal

Spiritual Setting: Today we shall place ourselves before the Cross or before the Eucharist, contemplating both the damage that our sins have caused upon the lovable body of Jesus and His poverty which attracts and invites us to imitate it.

Petition: Facing this sorrowful Ideal, what else can we ask for but love, and to imitate it — and contemplating such extraordinary poverty, what but detachment from everything that is not Him?

Response: To remain the whole day in contemplation of this Ideal, drinking it and inhaling it, trying to imitate Him in His suffering and in His poverty.

You are my Ideal, Jesus of my soul! Who has been my Ideal up until now, and Who will it be up until the last moment of my life? But You are not an ideal forged by the imagination; You are not a fictitious or vain ideal; You are a fulfilled Ideal that greatly supersedes everything the mind has ever seen, and all that the human mind can comprehend.

O my Ideal, my Jesus, my Treasure! Who could ever recount Your charm and your appeal? Who can explain that Divinity that permits Itself to be transparent in You, and attracts, fascinates, enraptures, and moves us?

Today I am going to slowly spell Your name … to look and stare at You… to frequently think about Your riches and Your charm.… I will enjoy You today, inhaling and exhaling You, covering You up in my suffering and my tears; enveloping You in that fire that devours me, so You do not experience coldness, my Beloved, but that You may rest within the warmth of my heart.

Today I shall see You in many different ways. As a Child? How delightful! … In Your first word.… What could it have been? Love! … In Your first steps that made violets sprout up from the earth? … In Your first tears that cried out, "Heaven!"

And when You were more grown up…
what a delight! Stepping barefoot upon the sand
of the desert, thinking about — O my Love! —
about my inconceivable aridity!

And later, that purity! those glances! …
such features… such a Heart.… What an attraction! … What a divine and saintly ensemble!

Further on, with the light of intelligence
upon Your forehead and divine rays from Your
Heart, astonishing all who heard You in the
Temple.

And back in Nazareth: labor, prayer, obedience… silence and martyrdom.

What would You dream about, my Jesus,
except to make suffering loved?

And in the desert… and Your preaching
that captivated, always choosing the mountains,
for You were a little Lamb… and Your miracles
… and Your modesty… and Your humility? O
and how this captivates me!

And the madness of the Cross… and Your
scourging and Your thorns… and Your agony…
and Your triumph… and Your desolation and
Resurrection… and Your Ascension and Your
heaven… and Your heroic virtues and the Eucharist and Your frenzies of zeal… and Your fire
and Your unequaled purity… and Your suffering, O Jesus, Jesus! And Your *love* — is this not
celestial? Does it not carry us away, captivate
us, and drive us mad?

Yet among all these multiple charms, which is the one that prevails most sweetly upon my heart?

Seeing You *upon a Cross,* my adorable Jesus!… There, there is where You often await me, to nail Yourself to me.… Do not delay, Lord, here I am at Your feet awaiting that happy moment!

Second Meditation

I contemplate You red with blood and dying for me, O Jesus, most pure Ideal of my soul! If, giving my life, I could save Yours! But it is necessary that my Treasure should die to give me the life of grace and of love.

My heart breaks upon contemplating that innocent Body broken, but *it is my own doing*, and I tremble upon contemplating it! But, nonetheless, since I have been the cause of Your suffering, I wish to console You… and with my breath… and with my voluntary sacrifices, and with all the tenderness of my heart, today I want to bring You solace.… I will never offend You again, my Jesus, and from now on I will give You only caresses… the best of my soul, my vitality, my entire being, hiding You from Your enemies deep in my heart.

That pierced forehead — I am going to soothe it with all my tenderness!

Those locks, soaked in blood — I will kiss them lovingly, a thousand times!

I will remove Your crown, and I will set it on my head, because the thorns are *only for me*… for You, happiness, not suffering; this is for me.

And that wounded Heart… and that volcano of love, and that wound… that fire! … Jesus, Jesus, what can I tell You?

Why is Your Body so cold, if Your Heart burns? I am going to warm You with my love… but burn me, Jesus, with Yours.

My heart breaks, my Jesus… let me rest while contemplating Your suffering.… But did You rest?

THIRD MEDITATION

O my Jesus, I want to cover Your nakedness with blood, and erase my ingratitude with suffering. I will be Your Calvary so that You may sacrifice Yourself upon it. I will also be your Cross, but a cross of honey and of flowers; a cross of virtue that does not hurt You, my Love.… On the contrary, it could be a balm that cures Your pain, and a comfort that enlivens Your love.

Do not suffer any longer; that is what Your children are here for! O Ideal that I pursue — of purity, of humility, of suffering, and of poverty! What will I say to You? That today before I leave, You may grant me at least one of these heroic and perfect virtues that You practiced, in order to breathe in its fragrance. Which one of them are You going to give me, Jesus of my soul? Answer me, my Love.

"Today I will give you My poverty, which I practiced from Bethlehem to Calvary... naked in the manger and upon the Cross! Lacking in clothes, food, and drink... in honor and praise... esteem and love... always forgotten and abandoned.

"Lacking in consolation, and rich only in humiliation, wounds, scorn, and disdain from My crib to the Cross.

"Poor in spirit, I say, inasmuch as I referred everything to My heavenly Father, giving back to Him all the treasures He communicated to My most holy soul.

"Always poor and even yet poorer in the Eucharist.... In the tabernacle, which is My delight, I am even yet poorer than in the manger and upon the Cross, for I have not even allowed Myself any movement.

"In how many tabernacles am I poor, naked, abandoned, helpless, insulted, crucified, without witnesses and without comfort?

"In the Eucharist I receive everything out of charity.... Four planks form My dwelling, and no brilliance announces My presence.

"This is My hidden crucifixion, My child, and if My Passion on Calvary moves you so, how much more should My Eucharistic passion en-amor you?

"Here in the Eucharist, My poverty is com-plete and perfect; My love for that virtue has driven Me to the point of hiding My Divinity and the splendor of My glorious humanity.

"Here I strip Myself of every liberty and exterior movement, of every possession and ev-ery domain. I find Myself in the Eucharist, cloaked and hidden under the sacred species, awaiting even the substance of the Sacrament from the charity of men.

"So then, My child, to become a saint one *must be poor,* preferring to have a little rather than a lot, less rather than more, taking Me as a model on the Cross and in the Eucharist."

RESPONSE

Yes, only Beloved of my soul, on the Cross and in the Eucharist, and in all Your precious life of poverty and suffering, You are the *Divine Ideal* that overwhelms my being.

Like You, I shall say to those who have pity on me, "Do not cry for me." I have a celestial Treasure, and that is enough for me. It is Jesus, *a poor Jesus* — so poor is He that He boasts of not even having a stone upon which to rest His head.

My richness is a bloodied Jesus, buried out of charity!

Thorns and hard nails are His property, and this shall be mine.

I desire to be like Him, unknown and despised, slandered and humiliated.

Blood and virtue, I need nothing more to cover myself! Slave and Victim. To be less… to crucify my ego… to dismember my will… to renounce myself completely; to kill my self-will, and even to be poorer than poverty itself, that is my longing.… In this manner I shall resemble this Ideal that I have engraved in the depth of my soul with flaming characters.

O good Jesus, my hope and rest for my spirit! Grant that my love for You may be *insurmountable… inseparable… singular,* and *insatiable*.…

Saintly Virgin, obtain this for me, from this Jesus Whom you contemplate, enraptured in heaven. Amen.

24

HOLY HOUR

My Lord and My God

Spiritual Setting: To see, to look, and to return to gaze upon that consecrated Host, and obeying the Holy Father's request, repeating with all the ardor of our hearts: *"My Lord and my God,"* and slowly savoring these very sweet words.

Petition: To ask, with a burning heart, that this Lord, this God, truly be ours, possessing us, absorbing us, making us divine.

Response: If He is completely ours, we will always and everywhere be His, and *only His, through pure love.*

You are twice mine, my Eucharistic Jesus, when I contemplate You in the sacred Host, which is my delight, my treasure, my own life! … *You are my property*… I am the owner of the Word made man… Jesus, mine? … A Lord, a true God, *mine?* … Have I duly considered this? … And to be mine… so that my lips can repeat this — that He is my own — before Him in His presence, what does Jesus do? He renews the action of His Passion, offers the same sacrifice of the Cross in every Mass…. He is incarnate…. He redeems… and He dies for me.

A profound humility propelled Jesus to renew His Incarnation and the actions that took place in His holy Passion, in the Mass, because the sacrifice offered upon the altar *is no other sacrifice* than the same sacrifice of the Cross.

Every time that Jesus sacrifices Himself, *He gives me life*, dying mystically for my love; this is what it costs Him *so that I can call Him mine…* to shed His Blood, delighting in His crucifixion.

During His Passion, Jesus shed His Blood, and that precious Blood fell upon His executioners, upon the ground, and on the rocks. The populace had their hands and their faces tinged with that divine Blood; but far from being purified, they were hardened in evil, while if Jesus had sprayed their souls, they would have been converted.

how many benefits we would receive! Nothing is denied us in those moments, because it is Jesus Himself Who *asks*, and Who *offers Himself*… Who *adores* and Who gives *thanks*…. His inexhaustible merits are what make the claim; His Passion, His Blood, and His wounds have an unlimited virtue and worth.

It is then when we pay all of our debts, and *we give more than we can even receive*… the Body of Jesus, the Blood of Jesus cry out asking for graces and mercy "and everything that we ask for in His Name shall be granted to us."

This is the supreme moment to ask for pardon, and blessings, and crosses and favors. Let us also gaze upon the Father in union with Jesus, and let us expect any sacrifice, for at His side, everything is sweet and gentle, everything smooth and delightful.

How this gaze of faith, of thanksgiving, and of holy union pleases Him! A gaze that thrills the heavens, makes the Father smile, pleases the Father and *disarms Him*, because we present Him Jesus, His delight, His Word, His only Son, all His Love.

RESPONSE

O *"My Lord and my God"* Who is really present before our eyes in that Immaculate Host! Innumerable hosts of angels surround Your throne!

We are kneeling in the midst of pure spirits that are joyful around Him! Cherubim and Seraphim cover their faces as they contemplate You! They consider themselves unworthy of even being in Your presence, and I, Lord, what should I do? … They contemplate You with their untarnished intelligence. I, I, Your poor creature, I introduce You into my body and into my soul, astounding them, and *I call You mine*, and You truly are this, with a union that does not exist even in heaven.

Just *to be mine*, You became incarnate in Mary, You humiliated Yourself to the limit, and You died upon a Cross.

Just to hear from my coarse lips that *You are mine*, You remained until the end of time in a consecrated Host! One of Your greatest pleasures is to make man happy, limiting Yourself to become his property…. Well, come then, *"My Lord and my God,"* I open my arms and the depths of my heart to You. I do not need to touch You in order to recognize You as Saint Thomas did; *I believe* and I will fall on my knees, thrilled, before any tabernacle, repeating a thousand times these words that drive me mad, that touch me, and constrain me and sanctify me: *"My Lord and my God!"*

Mary, Mistress and Mother of God! Give me all your virtues so I may, without blushing, call Jesus Eucharist: mine. Amen.

25

HOLY HOUR

The Three Nests of Jesus

Spiritual Setting: Let us see Jesus, peaceful and tender, Who comes near and says to us, "My child, look what a beautiful meditation I put before you today: the altar on which I sacrifice Myself... the tabernacle in which I hide Myself... and the monstrance in which I manifest Myself... that is, the most complete sacrifice ... the most profound humility... the most sublime manifestation."

Petition: For the good of our souls, we shall ask the Holy Spirit for His light to submerge ourselves in these three meditations.

Response: To transform ourselves through sacrifice, silence, and union with Jesus on a living altar, tabernacle, and monstrance, not separating ourselves from Jesus, for even an instant during the week.

"My child, your heart must be an altar upon which the innocent Victim constantly sacrifices Himself for the sake of the world. I have continued My Eucharistic life in three abodes: on the altar, in the tabernacle and in the monstrance, and I want you to be all three of these things for Me, because I have a hunger for your soul, because I want to live closely united with you.

"I want to repeat that word on the altar of your soul: *Ecce venio*… and to be sacrificed there, bathing you in My warm Blood, fruitful and life-giving… but if My life is given upon the altar, in the tabernacle, and in the monstrance, *it is not consumed there.*… It is eager for another end, and that is your heart.… It is, My child, *the heart of humankind.*… I do not sacrifice Myself upon the altar for any reason other than to *come* to die in your heart.

"I do not remain in the tabernacle for any reason other than *to arrive* in your heart.

"I do not raise Myself in the monstrance for any reason other than to descend into your heart.… Then if I desire to live within you, must you not be an *altar, a tabernacle,* and a *monstrance* for Me? Must not your heart be an altar on which I sacrifice Myself… a tabernacle in which I hide Myself … a monstrance in which I manifest Myself?

"Be then My altar, holy and free of every stain so that you may constantly remind yourself that 'No one has greater love than this, than to lay down one's life for a friend,' and if you are My altar, you will continually experience the sacrifice of the Incarnate Word within yourself… and the most intense fire of His love.

"But if I sacrifice Myself in you and for you… you, child of My Heart, what will you do for Me? Tell Me without hesitation… which incense are you going to burn in My honor? Will you be generous in consuming all the defects and affections that tie you to the earth and that impede My union? … Oh, and how many grains of incense, of which you know well, beloved soul, can you sacrifice in My honor? Will you deny it to Me?

"If I expire daily in your heart, will you not die inside of Mine?

"Should it not be sweet for you, remembering My suffering each moment? … Should it not be easy for you to sacrifice everything for My sake, when you see Me within yourself, on My altar — which you are — sacrificing everything, even life itself — for you?

Ah, My child! Why do I always have to ask you for what, by so many titles, belongs to Me, and why do you not fly, in the intensity of your love, to sacrifice yourself with all you possess, in union with Me?"

"If your heart is My altar, I also want it to be the tabernacle in which I hide.... My child, noise does not please Me.... The brilliance and radiance of the world do not attract Me. I am at ease only in the silence of a pure and sacrificed soul. *Let us live there only the two of us for ourselves, all alone....* I will cure your wounds with My most precious graces, and you will alleviate Mine with your love and with your unknown sorrows.... *I shall be your sweet secret....* I will guard your soul, mysteriously communicating with it.

"My dear child, you shall listen to Me if you are My silent tabernacle, and I will say to you, 'Learn from Me, for I am meek and humble of heart.'

"Even if you could gain the whole world, could you possess anything more than the Creator of the world?

"I will be your bounty, your riches, your happiness, your treasure, and even if you would direct your flight towards all the winds of the sky, even if you would excavate the most profound depths of the earth... even if you would survey the waves of the ocean, neither heaven, nor earth, nor the ocean would give you what you possess by being My tabernacle.... If your heart is where your treasure is, ask also for that Treasure to be always where your heart is.

"I want your glory to always be *interior*, that it might be Myself... and if He, Who is the beauty of heaven, hides Himself under these mysterious appearances, and these same appearances are hidden when He hides Himself in you — then you, poor little worm of the earth — should you not immerse yourself in Me, hide yourself, forget yourself, and lose yourself forever from sight without ever finding yourself again?

"The tabernacle is My heaven upon earth. Will you be this for Me: ... a pure and limpid sky, adorned with the stars of all the virtues?

"A life of intimacy with you is all I desire, and what greater intimacy if you shall be nearer to Me than the very darkness that envelops Me?

"O yes, My child, I love you so much that even the altar seems to be far away, and this is why I want you to be My tabernacle; but no, it is still not enough; I desire to come even closer, closer to you."

Third Meditation

"You will always be My monstrance — that is, you will be touching, in direct contact, with the Beloved of your soul! But is this the only thing I ask of you? What do I mean when I say, 'When I am lifted up from the earth, I will draw everything to Myself'?

"And so it is: If I descend into your heart, it is not only to give you a new life… to manifest Myself externally in the whole of your behavior… it is to produce the divine fruit of perfect virtue… it is to make Myself transparent through you… to diffuse a divine likeness in your soul and to be resplendent in every one of your actions.

"My child, many souls receive Holy Communion and do not know how to imitate Me in their sweetness, in their patience, in their humility… in their self-denial and love for mortification, and they hide a Jesus — obedient-until-death — in the bottom of their hearts and that obedience does not ever reveal itself in the accomplishment of their duties…. They carry a crucified Jesus in their souls and they run away from even the shadow of the Cross!

"In the Eucharist I arrive at the ultimate limits of love, and when I am offended in this Sacrament, man reaches the ultimate limits of ingratitude.

"Do not let this happen in your soul, My child! Let the Eucharist be everything for your heart, transforming yourself into it, so as to attract…. When you breathe, let your air be the Eucharist! When you eat and drink, let it be your daily bread and the fountain of living water! … When you walk, let it be your life! When you think, let it be your truth! … When you speak, let it be your word! … When you love, child, let this Eucharist be your love, all your love!

"To desire the Eucharist is the beginning of true life… to participate in it is the crowning of the soul's efforts, and to persevere in the Eucharist is perfect happiness upon earth.

"Be, then, My altar, My tabernacle, and My monstrance, where I sacrifice Myself, hide Myself, and manifest Myself."

RESPONSE

O Jesus of my soul! What condescendence, what generosity and what love You have for Your poor creature! What can I tell You, Beloved of my heart, but that I only desire to please You? I will then be Your altar, Your tabernacle, and Your monstrance, living, pure and recollected, in these holy thoughts.

How easily I will make You the sacrifice of my passions, and how sweet suffering will be for me, if I remember that my heart is the altar upon which Your Blood streams every moment!

How I will love the loneliness and the silence of soul, a quiet and lonely life, if I recall that my heart is the tabernacle where You hide Yourself.

And how I will desire to sacrifice myself and to imitate You, my adorable Jesus, so that

You appear in me, as I disappear!

Ah, my Lord, grant me what You are asking of me, and ask of me whatever You wish.

If the Eucharist is my consolation, who will be able to afflict me? If it is my happiness and my bliss, who can disturb me? Let it come, Lord, to fill my existence and let all my sighs be only for a consecrated Host!

Obtain for me this grace, Virgin Mary, from the Holy Spirit. Amen.

26

HOLY HOUR

I Look at Him, and He Looks at Me

Spiritual Setting: Today, with living faith, we shall experience the gaze of Jesus surrounding our whole being, and with clean, humble, and contrite souls, we lift up our eyes encountering those of Jesus, losing ourselves in His tenderness.

Petition: Today we shall ask for purity and humility, especially to see Him, for only through these virtues is one able to sustain the gaze of Jesus.

Response: A very lively and ardent presence of God, enkindled by His glance, and stored up in recollection and love.

First Meditation
He Looks at Me

My Jesus, I see You, and visibly I contemplate only a white consecrated Host... but my faith tears the veils with which Your charity covers You... My soul tears apart this cloud of humility in which You hide Yourself... and then I encounter Your glance that sees with a look that knows and magnifies everything... with the tenderness of a thousand mothers, with the unique love of God!

You look at me, Jesus, and those glances make me feel faint from love, but not with any kind of love, but with the kind of love from which the Seraphim must burn, and that melts even the stones themselves, *except me* Lord, rough and unworthy as I am!

He looks at me and communicates *life* to me... *warmth... happiness... peace!* A single glance of Jesus in the Eucharist infuses purity... humility... love.

Those pupils, when they look at you, copy heaven and divinity in souls.... The Father, the Holy Spirit, and the Word itself are there.

One of His glances is enough to make saints of the chosen ones.

And when those eyes, jeweled with tears, look at me, what shall I say? ... I wish to die? O no! This is what the soul desires, but no! To wipe them, I would rather choose to *endure, suffer*, and *sacrifice* myself a thousand times!

Certainly, for is it not our ingratitude that makes them flow with an infinite tenderness!

Do not look at me through Your tears, Jesus, Jesus, because I would die of pain.... Look at me smiling and pleasant... but as long as You look at me, look at me as You well please! Beloved of my soul, look at me in any way You wish, because then heaven covers me.

You also look at me, Jesus, from that consecrated Host of my life, with *entreating* looks; and this, could a child of Your love endure this without melting from love, without throwing herself into sacrifice, without dying of zeal? Impossible! It is a weight that annihilates, a tenderness of the Lord that propels one toward any martyrdom for His love.

Neither do I want You to look at me sadly, Happiness of the angels, because then my heart breaks. Pain, sadness and tears! This is proper for Your children who ardently desire to give You souls. But You, my Treasure, will have only rest, lullabies of tenderness, and songs of love from Your child.

SECOND MEDITATION
I Look at Him

I look at You and fall into ecstasy contemplating Your elegance... Your hidden virtues... Your attributes... Your beauty... Your multiple charms... Your loves and Your sorrows.

I look at You, O my heaven, in the Eucharist, and remain caught in the nets of Your beauty... of Your splendor... of Your Cross!

I look at You and You embrace me with Your breath, with Your perfume and celestial love.... I look at You again, and Your purity inebriates me, perfuming my whole being.

I look at You, Jesus, my adorable Jesus, and Your humility attracts me... overcomes me and enamors me, making me vehemently desire scorn, calumny, and the curses of the world, feeling happy, even in the small humiliations of every day.

I look at Jesus and His suffering attracts me irresistibly... and His Cross drives me mad, and I enthusiastically stretch out my arms to suffering because His nails are my nails, and His Passion, my passion.

I look at Him and His Divinity absorbs me... it carries me and elevates me from the earth and from myself and lifts me up to celestial regions.... I look at You and my heart cannot but tremble with love; a very pure, divine and scorching love that burns me, that enflames me, melting and consuming me in such a growing fire.

O yes, yes, my Jesus, I look at You and I forgive.... I look at You and I humble myself, and I sacrifice myself, and I loathe myself, and I desire martyrdom with passion, and scorn with frenzy — only to resemble You.

Ah, my Jesus, my Divine Word, my Lord and my God, here present! As I contemplate You, how many things happen to me which have no explanation because they take place in the very substance of the soul? ... You know them and this is enough for me.

THIRD MEDITATION
The Two of Us Look at Each Other

O yes, Jesus, Jesus of my soul! Both of us will look at each other, and the hours will fly without our being aware of it.... We shall look at each other today... we shall look at each other always, without ever taking our eyes from one another, with those glances of the soul that say everything, silent and mute... with those glances that intuit... that understand, that fuse two hearts into one only heart, Jesus, and this one must be Your own Heart, is it not so?

Do not ever look at me with anger, Lord.

O no! I wish Your gazes to be as those of a little Lamb Who forgives… or of a Dove Who commiserates… or of a Child Who attracts… or of a Crucified Who enraptures!

I want You to look at me with sweetness… with mercy… with pardon… with love!

But what is this that I am saying! For those pure and divine eyes, O my Jesus, cannot look otherwise, and much less upon His children. Is this not true, my Jesus?

They are never angry, they predict forgiveness and invite us to have confidence; they bless, they have pity and they love. Such is their language: love, love and only love! And this will also be my language, Jesus of my heart — from now on. I promise this to You. With the eyes with which I see You, drinking in Your life, I shall see my neighbor, having pity on him, forgiving, forgetting, overlooking! All of my glances shall be pure and full of charity, like Your own. How could they involve pride, if they are reflecting Him Who is humility? … I shall be full of love, Jesus of my soul, so as not to blush when I seek Your eyes: give me virtues, many of them — which will sprout from my heart, only within the warmth of Your glances! O yes, my Jesus, as the rays of the sun penetrate the earth and, as they say, form the precious stones — the silver and the gold — in this manner Your glances, Lord, dwelling in poverty and humility, can produce virtues and celestial treasures.

How very rich is the glance of a God-man, of my beloved Jesus, which makes everything that it reaches fruitful! Simply by looking at Peter, He extracted sin's poison! ... With those eyes He looked at Saint Matthew, at Mary Magdalene, at the good thief, at so many sinners, sanctifying them, and He looks at me to convert and to purify me.

O those glances of Jesus that wound like darts, always producing graces, that just by resting over the soul, enrich it!

O Jesus, where Your love is, there are Your eyes! ... O Jesus, look at me with those glances that create the chosen ones and the saints!

Response

O Life of my life! You have looked at me... I have looked at You.... We have looked at each other, uniting our pupils and our souls! What more can my lips say, if my eyes tell You everything?

I will say to You what Mary said to You: "Why have You looked upon Your lowly servant? You have led me to Your love and have preferred me over so many souls, without my being worthy of it." What can I say? That my heart falls into ecstasy at Your glance... that it transforms me... that it melts me, and that I clearly realize that when You look at me, my misery disappears… my spirit is purified… that it strengthens me in my weakness… that the practice of virtue becomes easier… that I desire to be a martyr… that I flee from the earth… that I come nearer to heaven!

But I also know that Your eyes are hidden only within poor and humble souls, so I desire to be poor and I shall not go away from here until You grant me the gift of humility to hide those eyes in the bottom of my soul, in the reliquary of my unworthy heart.

Mother of Jesus, and also my mother, since you were reflected in the divine pupils of our Lord as nobody else has ever been, grant that when my eyes close to the vision of this world, they might find themselves immediately under the gaze of your Holy Son, as well as your own. Amen.

27

HOLY HOUR

It Is You

Spiritual Setting: Today I shall see the Lord with a Host in His hand, and showing it to me, He says, "Do you see it? I am the Bread of life, and whoever eats this shall never die."

Petition: Jesus, always give us a hunger for this Bread of life that contains true Life, because we wish to nourish ourselves with its purest substance.

Response: If all of the gifts He has given us seem small to Jesus, and He Himself *even becomes a gift*, everything must also seem small to me, and I will myself become a gift, offering myself to His Will without reserve.

It is You... but, O my Jesus! Tell me, what do You call Yourself in the Eucharist?

"I am the Bread of life.... Such is My name, My child, upon this altar — *the Bread of life*, and whoever eats of Me, shall never die...."

O my Lord! The angels would have called You "Word," "Jesus," "God," but *"Bread"*? Only You, my Lord, only Your thirst for humility and the plan of Your love could have made You descend to such a point, descend to such a degree....

O yes! I feel that You are in that consecrated Host... because Who could ever touch my soul and make me thrill with such love? It is undoubtedly You, my Beloved, my powerful attraction, my celestial, holy, and divine Bread!

It is You and only You, here, at the foot of the altar, illuminating the most hidden recesses of my spirit, making me *know myself* and *loathe myself*. Who is it that can teach me humility? Who, but Him Who made Himself food to cure my pride?

O yes, my Jesus, Victim of love for man! You alone can be the One Who from Your throne can communicate to me the ardent desire for suffering that consumes me! ... You alone can propel my poor soul to union with You as a voluntary victim, a happy slave, for the love of Your abasement!

Isn't it true that You always point out the Cross and heaven for me? ... Isn't it true that You are the Bread of life Who, upon coming to my soul, anoints it with an angelic fragrance that is called PURITY? ... Isn't it true, my Heaven, my Sun and my Light, that You sparkle in the depth of my spirit, burning me, melting me, absorbing me, making me divine?

Who can it be Who does all of this but the Powerful, the Omnipotent, the Lover and the Loved One of my soul? O Eucharistic Jesus! O Bread of life Who begets living crosses! Who are You but the very charity that is displayed in the muddy and ill-smelling pond of my poor heart? Who are You but that Sun of which I have been speaking, that dries everything up... that Fire which consumes everything... and that Light whose rays do not become soiled passing through the marshes?

O Jesus, my Eucharistic Jesus, adorable Word of my life! What could my soul give You that would please You? Please tell me because I am dying to please You!

If You are the One to give so many things, should I not give You everything that I possess?

"Yes, it is I, My child, it is I who gives you all things and Myself with them!

"It is I, and when dealing with mankind, all of My gifts seemed so small to Me, *that I Myself became a gift*, in the Bread of life, to satisfy My loving desire to be near! Just as the sun appears with new beauty each day, so I come to your soul each day as glorious and beautiful as if I were coming only a single time.

"Mary received My passive Body within her, and you receive the impassive and celestial One…. Mary bore the Man of Sorrows, and you bore the Son of God crowned in glory…. It is I Who have realized these wonders of mercy.

"And for what reason have I come to live among you? Know, My children, that I have come to reinforce your love with virtue.

"My beloved children, I said, will have a powerful means to fly towards perfection, to know Me and to study Me, *tracing Me in the depths of their souls.* How they will study My hidden virtues… by imitating Me! How easy the virtue of humility will be for them after seeing My limitless humility, not only in the Sacrament, but also upon entering such poor hearts, in such unenlightened souls, in bodies so full of misery!

"How easy it will be for them to practice the virtue of meekness under the influence of

My most tender love living with them!

"How beautiful will their love for their neighbor be, looking at Me, the Bread of life, feeding both the just and the sinners!

"After having received Me crucified in your souls, My children, who will experience the bitterness of penance, of mortification, and of sacrifice?

"How very urgently you will experience the need to imitate My life in this *Eucharistic Cenacle*, in this abode that My love, *and only My love* has set upon the earth, where I desire to remain in your company!

"But what will you give Me in exchange? Be like My Mother, who, in the midst of all her greatness, saw only her own frailty and nothingness. It is necessary that you become like her, if not in dignity, truly in virtue; it is necessary that with every step you say, 'Behold, I am the handmaid of the Lord,' accepting a life of sacrifice and humility only for love of Me.

"You will not lack anything as long as you are with Me, but I demand a very precise response."

Third Meditation

"I desire a very delicate union with My sorrowful Heart; I desire hidden virtue of the type that the world does not know and in whose perfume I delight. I desire charity, purity, holiness: this is the reason that I have come to this place, the Tabernacle, to find solace in the midst of pure hearts that are not hindered by pain.

"What more can I do for these souls that I love so much?"

O Jesus of my whole soul! Certainly You cannot do any more for these souls than giving Yourself to us in this adorable Sacrament together with all You possess.

You have arrived… it is You…. You triumphed over our coldness, tepidity and ingratitude, with Your inconceivable charity! Your splendors fill this altar; one can breathe the air of heaven…. O yes! You occupy the hearts of every one of us; it is You… it is You!

What will we give You in exchange?

Love, love, love! No more detached and weak response! No more routine or spiritual laziness! These hearts, from now on, will be an oven of love, a beacon, a volcano of charity, reflecting a living, pure, immaculate and holy Host.

"This is what I want, My children, this is what I desire: to find My delight in all of you. I wish to nurture you with My substance… enliven you with My warmth… give you life with My life… relief with My Blood… light from My eyes… breath from My mouth… fire from My

Heart! ... Only in Me will you find liberty without obstacle... unclouded truth... the font of holiness.... I come to paralyze Satan's reign among you, because without Me *you can do nothing!* Therefore, what great purity of conscience must reign among you, what a lively presence of God, what a great spirit of sacrifice, what kindness in small things, because one does not reach perfection except by working specifically on each virtue!

"What unity, what obedience, what poverty, and above all, what purity and what love!

"'I am the Bread of life,' the food of those who love Me.

"'The Word has been made flesh!' This is Mary's glory.

"'The Word has made Himself bread.' This shall be Our glory."

Response

O Jesus, Eucharistic Jesus! What is it that You desire? My blood, my heart, my life, my hopes, my honor, my affections, my whole being? What, Lord? ... to sacrifice to You this very moment? What can I deny You, infinite Good, if I am Yours without reserve? ... What can be denied to the One we love? Ask, Lord, because what could You want that I would not wish, that I would not give to You? … To crucify me? … Yes, I want You to crucify me… To give me Your bitterness to drink? Your chalice is delightful to me when You place it on my lips! To submerge myself in the most cruel abandonment and desolation? That is what I deserve, my Jesus, without being worthy of it: to live suffering from the absence of my only Love.

Life, death, what does this matter for one who is Yours and desires only Your Will?

All labor and humility, what are they for a handmaid?

All pain and suffering, what are they for a victim?

With You and in union with You, what can I fear?

It is You alone Whom I love, and nothing else besides You. You alone are my Companion, my Treasure, my Loved One! … If it is You Who presents the Cross to me, then let a thousand of them come, for I, thrilled and grateful, shall press them against my heart, telling them full of love: they are You… they carry You; it is You… it is You in them, O my Jesus! And because of this the measure of my love will be to love them beyond measure!

Let all of this be so, Celestial Mary, so that my love will not remain mere words, but will be expressed in works of sacrifice. Amen.

28

HOLY HOUR

You Can Feel Him

Spiritual Setting: We will sit at Jesus' feet with Mary Magdalene, humbled and repentant, permitting our souls to be immersed in Him in this silence and solitude.

Petition: We shall ask Jesus-Host for the light and grace to know Him and to discount ourselves.

Response: What can we ask after this heavenly hour, but the very real presence of God, which will propel us to every mortification and sacrifice for His love.

You can feel Him… O yes, here you *can feel God…* you can inhale and breathe Him, filling this humble cenacle of the earth, impregnating the atmosphere with celestial perfume. This tabernacle bears the fragrance of Jesus; one enters here as if entering Jesus' innermost being; with that same respect… that same confidence… that same love. The light, the warmth, the fire of the Eucharistic Jesus fills everything, and thus, in this beloved enclosure, the thorns are roses… sacrifice is not felt… pain and martyrdom are sweet because they are suffered for His sake and in His intimacy.

If the altar is poor, Jesus is its richness… its most delicate embellishment. Without being fully aware of it, one enters into profound concentration and prayer because one leaves earthly things at the door, and the soul is engulfed in the possession of its Beloved.

Here — all alone, He and I — He, with all His greatness, and I with all my miseries — He, all fire; and I, burning in the midst of His divine Passion! … My darkness is lost in the midst of His light…, and my icy heart melts inside of His. Here my sins are forgiven and my sorrows — O! my sorrows are united to His own, giving them value.… How many treasures are enclosed in this holy place, consecrated through the presence of Jesus in the Blessed Sacrament! Heaven is here, because *He is here!*

I would not exchange these four walls for the most glorious palace on earth!

You can feel Him, yes… here the Lord can be felt… here He can be found… here the soul loses itself in His arms. It cries out contritely, is anxious to suffer, and *loves Him!*

Jesus inflames us in the nearness of that Holy Host. This is the enclosed garden, the place selected for divine appointments… for holy conversations… for divine loves.… Here, at the foot of this altar, the palpitations of the heart are also supernatural, desiring the possession of God, celebrating the Mysteries of the life of the heart with Him.

Here the tongue truly occupies itself only in praising… the eyes in crying… and the heart in loving the One Who is all lovable.… Here love grows and grows until it has no other wish or desire but the will of God. Here, Jesus of my soul, I love oblivion, scorn, and obscurity; and the world and worldly things are removed from my heart according to the measure that my spirit possesses You! You are the glory of my life, Eucharistic Jesus. I am happy here, consuming myself in Your presence like the candles on the altar.… I languish from the love of possessing You, with an insatiable hunger for a greater union and more sacrifices.

But why is it that we feel Jesus here? *Because of the emptiness of the soul, because the world is very far away,* because we have no witnesses and the solitude of the heart is complete.

And this is why my love grows according to the measure that I empty myself… that I humble myself… that I sink… that I lose myself in my unworthiness and in my nothingness.

My Eucharistic Jesus, I love You more now that I hide myself so that You may appear… now that I conceal myself so that You may reign… now that I am nothing so that You may be *everything.*

I love You more, much more, adorable Jesus… now that I have died to earth's vanities… now that, with Your grace, I have moved away from worldly things… now that I have renounced being something that was not trash… now that I have stood in the shade so that others could shine!

I love You more now that I keep my soul clean… now that I am voluntarily poor… now that I obey and crucify myself to please You.

Is it not true, my Jesus, that all of this is the fruit of solitude, and that at the foot of Your Sacrament one enjoys an intimacy that is unknown to the world because of its purity? Here, let me say it very near to You, Jesus of my life! Caresses and tenderness flow night and day in the midst of pain and tears…. Here my sighs burn You and Your glances scorch me…. Here I hand You my pain and You envelop me in Your love.

O Jesus, Eucharistic Jesus! In this silence and solitude that surrounds us, my heart bursts forth with all the fire of the love that You communicate to me, and which consumes me; and the burning lava of this volcano is transformed into madness, into delirium, into unspeakable tenderness.

O Eucharistic Jesus! Here I tell you my sorrows, my sins, my bitterness, the misery of my soul, and my feeble response.

Here, I also hear Your complaints, Your rebukes, Your desires, Your teachings and Your forgiveness. Mutually, we dry our tears from our souls, and the world ignores what only the angels contemplate.

I offer You my joys, I let You share in my sorrows, and You sweeten everything with Your touch.

Your wounds make me bleed, Your thorns prick me, and Your nails pass through me.

And the hours fly by in the intimacies of Him Heart to heart, and dawn comes before the Sun of my love sets.

And if I experience this celestial life, why is it that I sometimes desire persons or things that are not Him? … What is the benefit of filling myself with the smoke of human appreciation, vanity, and self-love, which — alas! — diminish Jesus' presence in my soul? During the nights of my spirit, why do I look for affections that are taken by the wind, piercing the heart?

Why build my nest in that which passes away and disappears, when here I have Him Who always is? O my God! I will no longer waste time on silly speculations and self-pleasure, in crazy illusions that stain the heart and hurt it vainly.

Why do I look for peace, for happiness, and joy outside of the Cross in all of its forms and why am I anxious to get away from the martyr-doms to which Jesus wants to subject my body and my soul?

From now on I will have no other aspira-tion than that of humbling myself more and more, and of suffering more and more.

The repose of my soul can only be realized in the Eucharist and in the Cross, and I vainly tire myself searching for *how to be more of Jesus* if it is not by crucifying myself constantly because of His love.

I will no longer look for my happiness in anything other than complete mortification and in that complete sacrifice of my entire being on the altar of purest love, unselfish and generous. I will not say, then, how much I love God *if I do not love mortification,* if I desire anything other than letting myself be crucified by God and by men.

My joy will be only in suffering, which has the virtue to purify and the grace to unite.

I will no longer waste time on theories of virtue, my Jesus, but I will hurl myself with ardor to be torn from myself and from everything I love to turn my heart into a living candle that burns its affections and desires in front of this altar.

I will not covet any treasure other than humility, scorn, disdain, and contempt of worldly things, non-existence, even to disappear from all their hearts, so that Jesus may occupy my place. My place is not upon the floor, but in the heaven of this consecrated Host: it is there where I will set my nest, deeply hidden in the Heart of my Beloved, there to learn silence, the interior life, and solitude, which bring so many benefits for the soul.

RESPONSE

O Jesus of all my soul! Here and everywhere You are my ALL.

Is it not true that I could never explain *the way I love You*? Is it not true that You are going to give me an ever more ardent love, with a lively desire to love always more? *I love You!* What a lovely word! And all the affections of my soul will always be for You.

O Eucharistic Jesus! What will I do with You, Passion of my soul, Continued Thought, Blood that runs through my veins, Breath of my life, Master and Lord of my whole being?

You undoubtedly already loved me from eternity.... I feel, Jesus, Jesus, that You preceded me, being mine before I was Yours! At the dawn of my life Your goodness already brightened my life, and now at the sunset of my life, Jesus, I ask that You bury me inside of Your eternal splendors. Here I feel that You have clung to and filled up Your poor creature. Then, why is it that I live — O! — if You die upon a Cross?

My Heaven... my Host... my Jesus! What could be *more mine* than You, my adorable Eucharist? I feel You more deeply within me than my veins, than my heart, than my soul! How can this be possible if You are a heaven and I am a mud puddle?

How is it that You reflect Yourself in this mud puddle? … How is it possible that You live in this pigsty? … How can You stand this corruption? Explain to me, O Lord, that which I cannot understand except as charity, compassion, and only as the LOVE of a God.

O Mary, celestial reliquary of Jesus' love! Help me to experience not only sacred love, but also the madness and the sorrows of the Cross. Amen.

29

HOLY HOUR

Here I Am

Spiritual Setting: Let us listen to Jesus, Who, bending down, with the sweetest accent, says to us, "Here I am.... I have arrived and I will never again depart."

Petition: Let us ask Him that we also never depart from Him through sin, through imperfection or tepidity, and to have us die before permitting such a disgrace.

Response: Recollection… that our life be an offering of all our actions to Him without ever losing sight of Him, and endeavoring so that our whole life will be a continual act of love.

"I have arrived, My child, overcoming infinite distances and solving every difficulty that stood in My way.... I have arrived here.... I have reached the loving end that I had in mind when creating this place for My solace.

"I have come to be with you, but do you know for what else I have come? *To ask you for your heart*... so that having your Treasure in the monstrance, you would have your heart there also... so that you could love Me with all your soul, with all your strength, but also with all your heart.

"This is the reason for My coming to the world: to look for man's heart, that is to say, the center of his tenderness, in which I have My delight.... I left heaven because I saw you were very far away, My child, and I contemplated you all alone without the Eucharist... because My love for you, poor little earthworm, impelled Me to come nearer, so the Word could take on flesh to give it to you divinized in the Sacrament of Love. I desired to live *near and inside* of you, and this is the reason I left My throne of Cherubim, and My pedestal of Seraphim. I have come to occupy, with great pleasure, this, My poor and silent dwelling-place upon the earth.

"Ah, dear child of My Heart! If you have loved Me for many years, I have loved you from eternity to eternity; your sins, your forgetfulness, and even your ingratitude were not — listen to Me — were not a reason to cool My love. I have loved you with an eternal love… in eternal charity have I loved you.

"I have arrived in this place, My child, to tell your heart that which I ask of you today: that My Passion and My martyrdom were not enough to satisfy My thirst for suffering, and I want you to continue doing what I can no longer do; that is to say that you suffer, that you endure, and that, being a victim in My union, you offer yourself with Me, for the sake of My redemptive plans.

"I desire to have here simple, poor, hidden and generous souls that have their delight only in sacrificing themselves in My honor.

"I tell you that I formed this holy place, My tabernacle, for us to be here *all alone… nearer* to each other… Heart to heart, communicating to you My *innermost being* in every heartbeat.

"*I have arrived* so that you may remain in Me, and so that your heart may have life, because in the same way that the branch cannot bear fruit if it is not attached to the trunk and to the root, you cannot do anything if you are not united intimately with Me, through the purity of your heart, interior solitude, and holy recollection.… Thus you will imitate Me more easily, crucifying yourself in union with Me, for there is no other way to become more spiritual than to mortify oneself."

SECOND MEDITATION

"Unite yourself with My soul, My child, with My spirit, with My merits, with My virtues, with My divine life, for this is the Sacrament of union with God.

"You must come out of your self-love and enter forever in Me; it is necessary that the eyes of your soul are always here, open to contemplate Me.... It is necessary that you bend your ear, *'Audi filia,'* in order to listen to Me; bend, O yes, bend the ears of your soul to My voice: 'Forget your father's house, because you shall be the object of the King's love.' Live in My presence; feed yourself with My life; rest, pure and humble, upon My Heart, listening to the soft and mysterious voice of love in this quiet and silent altar.

"When you arrive at My feet, humbled and pure, self-denied and recollected, you will understand many truths of self-knowledge, illuminated by the very light of God; you will touch the depth of your misery... you will cry for your failures... you will understand My predilection for you... and you will experience the fortitude and the peace of the Holy Spirit.

"A spiritual life is what I am pursuing for My beloved souls; a life of prayer, because all the power of saints sprouts from it; but to really lead a divine life, it is necessary that you give Me your heart, that you remain in Me, because, 'If you remain in Me,' I said on one occasion, 'and My words remain in you, ask for whatever you want and it will be done to you.'... 'If you love Me, you will keep My word, and My Father will love you and We will come to you, and make Our dwelling with you.'

"Courage, then, My children, for *I have arrived* to count your virtues and to compare your fervor, comforting Myself with your love, and suffering from your forgetfulness! ... I follow you with My glances, I have you printed in My pupils and your name is engraved upon My Heart... and when I see you approaching Me, to find breath and life, here at My feet, I will spill out My graces. I abound in tenderness, and I wish to bring you *nearer and nearer* to Him Who is your life, by means of perfect virtues, of constant humility and voluntary self-denial."

THIRD MEDITATION

"Why should I not tell My children, in loving confidence, what I desire? In this place, at the foot of the tabernacle, I desire more purity and humility, more self-denial and abnegation.... I want their souls to be divinized.... And how? With a hidden life in union with God, denying themselves, feeding themselves with virtues, and proving their love *with actions.*

"My child, uproot the bad weeds from your heart, and reach down into your heart until you achieve a void of yourself, a void which you must fill with Jesus. A loving child must not always stay the same size, I must say, but a loving child must always be LESS, leaving aside at every moment the bark of its self-love, of its affections, and its desires — even its own being — until its own personality, that is its ego, disappears — so that only *He Who Is* reigns in the soul, the soul's Eucharistic Jesus, absorbing everything and giving it life.

"It is necessary to free yourself from everything that is earthly, to be pure in actions and more simplified in love.

"At the foot of the altar you must be lost to yourself and absorbed in Me, conquered by My beauty, My goodness and My love.... You must let go of everything that is material, of your feelings, of the world, with your glance so purified that, penetrating through the natural darkness, it may candidly penetrate God's light.

"My love desires all this, My children, that same perfection in every soul who comes to kneel at My feet. This is why *I have arrived* not only at the steps of this altar, but in the depths of their hearts.

"I desire that they offer Me up to the Father with great purity of soul, with a very supernatural and loving intention, and with profound self-denial, uniting themselves lovingly to My own immolation.

"A glance, a sigh, will be sufficient, and an interior lifting up of the heart, a light touch of their souls with Divinity, an elevation of the spirit eagerly looking for Him Who is their everything, so that they may increase their intimate life with God, to Whom they must aspire with all their strength. Be always recollected, with a simple and natural recollection, practicing all the virtues, without anyone noticing it.

"Finally, take up your cross and follow Me. And what does it mean to take up the cross and follow Me? It consists *of coming out of yourself…* renouncing yourself… dying to any personal desire so *that only I* may live and reign in your soul. *This means to say NO to your yes, and YES to your no;* then you will have accomplished your vocation as victims, and given Me true comfort. This is what it means to crucify oneself… this is what it means to lose the old life and to come out of yourself to live within Me… so that I may live in you; this is the reason I left My throne of Cherubim to arrive at this altar so that I may live in you."

Jesus, Jesus, Jesus! What can I say? Only that I desire to please You and to sanctify myself with these celestial teachings that You give me today. I desire and I ask You for this true transformation into Yourself. I will happily study You in the delightful hours I spend at Your side, surmising Your desires and flying to accomplish them. I will remove distractions from my soul.... I will try to practice emptiness and solitude of soul, with holy recollection; I will be a voluntary martyr, renouncing myself with an ever more lively love that may surpass everything. All of this will form, within my spirit, that interior life that You demand of me.

My heart is Yours alone, Jesus. I shall live concealed inside of the consecrated Host which is my heaven, my life, my all, and be hidden, like the violet.

An interior glance, simple and pure, with every worldly dust and self-love shaken away, enclosing a tender prayer for sinners, will be the continual food of my adoration, when I have the happiness to come here.

O Jesus, how much do I love You! But ever since You have come to Your throne, this love in me is strange, grown up, fiery, immense. I love You, I love You, my Heaven, with Your own love, undoubtedly, and this is why my heart melts, kindled by such heavenly fire; turn it to ashes that a new life might be transplanted into it, another life, another soul, another being, making my life disappear, so You, Jesus of all my soul, may occupy the place of this poor child who was, but who is no more, because Another One has taken my place. Who can it be? … You know…. Who can it be, O my Treasure, my Beloved, my Life — *He Who came and stole all of my heart?*

Mary, Queen of my heart, now that I possess Jesus in my soul, grant that I may never let Him depart, that I close the door with the greatest love. Amen.

30

HOLY HOUR

Christmas

Spiritual Setting: Today we will approach the Manger with a very pure and translucent soul, empty and in interior solitude; there we will kiss the rosy temples of the divine Babe, and contemplate the movement of His lips, that quietly murmur, as if dreaming: "Eucharist!"

Petition: Seeing such poverty, humility, and mortification, what can we ask before the Manger other than these same virtues, falling in love with them?

Response: Love, love for that infant of the soul, for that rosebud, begging Him not to open His arms, because if He does, our soul will break into pieces.

The Eucharist was sown in Bethlehem. What else is the Eucharist but the wheat of the Chosen, the living Bread? Now, wheat is sown, is placed in the earth so it may germinate and ripen, until, once harvested, it is ground to make the bread.

When He was born upon the stable's straw, our beloved Word made flesh already prepared His Eucharist. That celestial wheat, thrown over the trampled straw, shattered and sterile, representing humanity, will be raised by Jesus, He will give us back our life and will make it fruitful in many virtues.… There He is sowing that *divine Grain*… the tears of love and the pain of a God-Child of a Child-God, will be — O my God — the moisture that will make it germinate! That precious Grain will become the model and the delight which will incline toward Calvary when mature, so that we may sow it.

Bethlehem is built upon a hill that looks toward Jerusalem, and when this ear bends toward Calvary it will be ground and put in the fire of suffering so it may turn into the Living Bread, into that Eucharist about which Jesus dreamed, anxious to feed us with it.

O divine Child, the thought of giving Yourself to us in this Sacrament, which we ecstatically contemplate, already formed Your delight from the Manger. How can we respond to that infinite love?

O Jesus of our whole soul! In our small-ness we find a way, and that is to feed You with virtues, with sacrifices and with love, as You feed us with Your own Body and Blood!

Come, precious Wheat, adorable Word, to grow in the soil of our hearts, so that growing with You, we will happily incline ourselves to-ward Calvary. This is what Your children de-sire: to be wheat in union with You, ground in any way for the good of souls.

Second Meditation

Jesus is a little Lamb; that is why He was born in a stable…. Ah, my Love! Just as the little lambs, He knew only His Mother. The first beat of His loving Heart was to offer Himself in sacrifice. "Father," He said in the depth of His soul, "the sacrifices and the victims of the Old Law did not please You, but You have given Me a Body, so now I voluntarily carry the world's crimes; here I am… *Ecce Venio.*"

And this little Lamb will grow next to His Mother, and she shall learn, forty days later, the secret of His immolation…. She will feed Him with her pure and virginal milk and shall keep Him until the day of the sacrifice! … Poor Mother! Those little eyes she now contemplates with emotion and which shine like the sun: she shall see them closed, coagulated with blood and tears unto death.... Those little ermine-white hands: she shall see them pierced not much later.... Those milk and honey temples that she now caresses with deep love: they will be pierced with pricking thorns.... That little mouth, now smiling, red as the poppies and carnations: it will be given gall and bitterness to drink.

But why remember suffering at the Manger, a place of happiness? We will only rejoice in the charms of Jesus.... Nonetheless, He is a Lamb, and the *character of a victim* will be always sealed upon Him; thus, on the first day of His public life, when seen by Saint John the Baptist, no other name could be found by which to designate Him, but the name of Lamb. *"Ecce agnus Dei qui tollit peccata mundi." This is the Lamb of God who takes away the sin of the world.*

And what began in Bethlehem is consummated upon the altar during the Mass; there we have both Bethlehem and Calvary; and in the consecrated Host we do not venerate a mere remembrance: not only Jesus' image, but the very same divine Child, our stalk of Grain, our Lamb, our Bread! ... In Bethlehem the same virtues shown to us in the sacramental state began. There Jesus hides His Divinity to have man become familiar with God.... There He covers His glory to later hide His humanity.... As a small Child He restrains His power with His weakness, chaining it later under the holy species.... The stable is not His, He sees it as an alms-offering, and later this celestial Child, this Word Incarnate, will ask man for a "dwelling place in which to live, … and a little flour for His Sacrament"!

O humility and poverty that attract us so! O Lamb without blemish! O Child — the mildness, sweetness, and heaven of our hearts! Life of our life! Come to our souls erasing all the sins of the world with Your purity. O Immaculate little Lamb, have pity on us!

Third Meditation

With the Eucharist, this Child of ours has come to counteract the words of Satan, with which he made our first parents fall, filling the world with incalculable harm.

"A Savior has been born to us," the angels announced to the shepherds in Bethlehem; that is to say, a new world, a divine restoration, has begun, and man will be happy now. A divine Sun will begin His race; He appears at Bethlehem and reaches His plenitude in the Eucharist.

The central point of Adam's sin, enclosed in the diabolic temptation, was summarized in these words, and in the feeling of pride that our first parents experienced by them: "You shall be like gods; you shall be like God," and they came to be like the beasts.

Well, truly the divine Child of Bethlehem

came to reproduce these words, to repeat Satan's words, but to accomplish them. Satan will be caught in his own snare. Yes, we shall be like God, because we will feed upon His Flesh and upon His Blood…. With this heavenly food the soul is transformed, divinized, and it changes its state, ascending to a more perfect union. A daughter of the country comes to be a queen when the king elects her as his wife. Jesus associates us to His Divinity in the Sacrament. Communion elevates us to a supernatural union and makes us participants in God's own nature, may I say, assimilating us to Him by the frequent participation of His adorable Body.

"You shall not die," Satan said, and the Child Jesus, the Savior of mankind, gives us a sure token of this in Communion: "Whoever eats My Flesh and drinks My Blood will live forever, and I will raise him on the last day." We shall then be immortal and this life is only a step to reach true life…. "You shall know everything," the devil said — evil, truly — but not good; but in Communion one drinks the divine knowledge of virtue, a science taught by the celestial Master: "I will no longer call you servants," Jesus once said, "but My friends, for a slave does not know what his master is doing. I have called you friends because *I have told you everything I have heard from My Father*" (John 15:15).

Here He is teaching us to love as His Father loved Him… and to sacrifice ourselves with the same charitable goals that He had… here He is showing us from the tabernacle how we must obey, how we must be poor, and pure, and holy. Here He is pouring out His benefits, teaching us to uproot vices and to practice virtue, the knowledge of the Cross, of silent suffering, of voluntary pain, of self-forgetfulness. Perfect and heroic virtues — where have we learned them except through Him? And that frenzied love, to love Him always more, of desiring to humble ourselves and to disappear, longing for suffering under any form for another's sake, this sublime doctrine in which the soul denies itself and takes up its cross — where did it come from?

And finally, the love that unites earth with heaven, that began with the Incarnation, that appeared in Bethlehem, that was burnished at Calvary, and that continues in saintly souls, especially in those who have embraced religious life; all of this infinite good and this supernatural order — to Whom do we owe it?

RESPONSE

O my Child! Heaven of my soul! What can I give You, what will You give me today? I will give You purity, and You will give me poverty, O yes, beloved Jesus of my life! Give me that pearl which I long for and covet at any price, to set it in my heart. I will give You kisses and You will give me *pain!* To be wheat, to be a lamb, to be a victim for Your love is what I *desire*.

O my lovely One, rosy-cheeked and beautiful! Give me the treasures of Your Cross, that the world considers madness and that I desire to love with all my strength; give me that Cross You dreamed about, that was Your delight since the Manger; give me oblivion, pain, and scorn, because the tender, pure, intense and immense love I have for You kills me, and I wish to imitate You to quiet its ardors.

O divine Word, Child of my soul, so white and ruddy! I feel You throbbing, being born and living in the midst of the straw of my cold heart. Child and man; innocent and with a perfect mind… with a heart that understands and that makes itself understood! Such little feet, such a forehead, such a mouth, such grimaces, such tears and smiles, what an ensemble, what a God-man, what a Savior of mankind, what memories that thrill me! O my Treasure! I love You with the most delicate tenderness, with the most intense ardor, and I desire to offer You my works, my sufferings, my blood and soul and heart, and a thousand souls and hearts conquered through the martyrdoms You wish to send me.

O happiest Mother, smother our Jesus with kisses and caresses in my stead. Amen.

31

HOLY HOUR

What Are You Telling Me?

Spiritual Setting: Today I see my Jesus Who, reclining near my heart, says to me with an enchanting voice, "What are you telling Me, My child?"

Petition: I will ask the Lord that I put everything I am going to say truly into action.

Response: Not to separate myself from Him today, pressing Him against my heart, taking care that while He is reclined upon it, there will never be even the smallest blemish in me.

"What do you have to say to Me, My child? Speak, I am anxious to listen to you... and to be lulled by your loving words. I am yours... and I have come to rest a little upon your poor but loving heart.... Do not fear.... Open your soul to confidence, for only one thing is necessary for Me: love, love, and only love."

O my Lord! My beloved Lord! Yes, rest Your precious Head with its crown of thorns upon my soul, and I shall venerate it with all my heart. Listen, Jesus, to the delirium of my love, and forgive me.

I can say nothing more than that I love You so much, that I am so happy at Your side... and that I forget all of my sufferings when I am right next to You. I tell You that my soul longs for these adorations and moments of heaven that I spend at the foot of this cherished monstrance, like a thirsty person longs for the fountain... like a sick person longs for health... like a poor man for a coat... like the blind man for the light... and all of this is little; the truth is that I am dying, my Jesus, to be with You, *only because I love You*.

I am also anxious to fly and come to prostrate myself here at Your feet, to take my breath in Your presence... life in Your Blood... light in

Your eyes… and courage, and grace, and pain, and fire from Your Heart.

I need the warmth of the Eucharist in order to live… the rays from my Sun, Jesus, to warm me…. Your glances, the rays from heaven, to be pure… Your heartbeats, to be holy.

I come here, my Jesus, to knock at the door of Your ever-vigilant Heart, to ask for light… grace… life… fire… love… and all the virtues to communicate them… and I guess, Charm of the Tabernacle, that You receive comfort from my love and that You rest within my suffering.

My soul is troubled, Lord, as long as it does not rest in You… and here, in You, it rests, absorbing sweet peace like a bee does honey.

O my Eucharistic Jesus! As long as You like me to say what I feel… what I suffer… what I desire… what I long for… and how I love You, I am also going to tell You what I need, what I do not possess, and what You are able to give me.

Second Meditation

I do not have humility, Lord… patience… self-denial… love for penitence… purity of intention… recollection… and the spirit of mortification…. Will You give them to me? I need to control my feelings and powers and to concentrate all of my affections in You.… I desire to untie, to loosen myself from everything that is earthly, to be very pure in my actions, taking away from my heart the world, matter, disordered affections; to come out from myself, Jesus of my soul, so as to enter forever into You.

I desire to build my world inside of You, to concentrate and remain in You, so as to live Your very life.

I want to drink You and breathe You crucified, with no movement other than Your will, with no thought other than to sacrifice myself for others, with no aspiration other than to love You and make You loved. I desire, Beloved of my soul, not to lose, in this holy place, even a syllable from Your mouth… nor a sound of Your voice, nor a palpitation of Your Heart… nor a single glance from Your eyes.

I desire — do you know what, Jesus of my hope? I desire more crosses… more suffering… more You.… This is what I desire, my Love! For this my soul thirsts, longing and hungry for more of You… for more pain!

Listen to me, my Heaven, Who are so very near me who loves You so: listen and see how I stretch my arms toward You, how I lift my heart, thirsty and anxious to love more, to suffer more for the Beloved.

Do You not hear the hastened beating of this heart where You are reclined? Do You not hear how day and night it cries out to You with-out ever tiring, *"More! More!"*

Behold, Jesus of my soul: I desire, O yes, more mortification that makes me resemble You…. I desire more purity so that I may be like You…. I ask You for more suffering to take on the features, the resemblance, the family likeness with the Crucified Whom I love so much.

I long for more bitterness, disappoint-ments, and martyrdoms… more pricking thorns, more illnesses, more sacrifices, scorn and dis-dain from the worldly. And do You know why, Jesus of my soul? Just to make a gift for You… just to please You, *just to comfort You!* But, above all, I ask You — I desire vehemently, ardently, and with tears, and cries, and blood — more love, even more love, because I would die for not loving You more, much more, infinitely more.

What would it cost You, my Lord and my God, to listen to me and give me — O my Jesus Word-Made-Flesh — a little piece of Your own Heart?

If you give me Your Blood… if You give me Your Life… Your Body, Your Soul, Your Di-vinity, Your whole Being in that consecrated Host, how could You not give me more love… an immense love… a heavenly love… Your own love that melts Your Heart, that burns it and yet does not dissolve it because You are God?

"Go on, My child, because My delight is to be among humankind… among the children of men.… Go on, because you please Me with your petitions, because it is the Holy Spirit Who has placed them in your soul. Ask and you shall receive… knock, and it will be open to you; trust, trust, because confidence is the last word of love; ask with humility, with simplicity, with purity and perseverance, and you will be heard. What else do you desire, child of My Heart?"

Lord, I would like to possess the tenderness of all hearts, to bring to You. I would like to have the caresses and virtues of holy souls to bring to You as a gift. I would like whiteness and light to receive You.… I would like millions of souls to consecrate to You.… I do not know what I desire in order to please You, Life of my soul; I think of heaven and it seems too small for You… and the thousands of hearts that are in the world, I think of them as a small drop to quench my thirst for glorifying You.

O Jesus, Jesus, Jesus! You understand me! … I, always longing and burning for Your nearness, am going to ask again that You give me more suffering, because I desire to be a victim… more purity, because I wish to be an angel… more humiliations, because I want to be holy… every day I wish to sever what is of excess, going deeper afterwards so as to form a void of myself which You are going to fill.

I desire, my Lord, not only to shape myself by coming down to the level of the earth that everyone may trample, not only to descend, to be a slave and to hide myself, for even so I would still be complete; I wish to go further than that to the point of disappearing from my own eyes, to the point of diminishing my ego, severing nature, being always less, for others' sake, and for Your glory.

I want a deeper interior and divine life… more light and graces, more Eucharist, O yes! Always more of it, without ever being satisfied. Jesus of my soul! I desire to transform myself into You, Beloved of my heart, more concealment and obscurity, *to come down, down* into the bottomless depth of my nothingness, more of the cross, more of the cross, so that finally, there will be more heaven afterwards… more unity, more divine embracing… more You, more You forever and ever.

Response

This is all I say to You, my Love, my Heaven, My Jesus! Because my duty claims me, I am leaving, but where my treasure is — that is to say, where my Jesus is — is where my heart will be.

So then, either I leave without my heart, or I am taking Yours. But as Your Heart cannot separate itself from You nor from Your Cross, we shall all go to love while suffering and to suffer while loving, for this must be my path through life.

What are You telling me, my Jesus? Are You going to give me Your Heart that is mine? If You give It to me, I will put Yours within mine, or mine within that oven of love so that there it might be purified, refined, and enhanced, soaked in Your charity. I will bring It back to You without any thorns, for this is the sublime task that heaven gave me in my good fortune. I will take them out one by one without hurting It, Jesus, curing Its wounds with the balm of my purity and of my love... My tears of repentance will wash It, and my ardent kisses will heal Its wounds. Give me that Heart, full of tenderness and mercy, and I will take my leave, Jesus; but even if my body is leaving, my eyes, that I leave at Your feet, will *tell You everything*, and will *give You everything*.

My mother! Every moment, tell Jesus everything that My loving soul has told Him. Amen.

32

CONTEMPLATION
(Good Friday)

All Alone with Him

Spiritual Setting: Today, with great respect and love, we will take Jesus' agonized and bloodied head in our hands, and thereby contemplate our sins and His love.

Petition: Lord, may I know You and myself as well.

Response: A very deep love for Him Who gave me life — and His own Life, so that I may imitate Him in His generosity.

I desire neither people, nor noise nor witnesses, but Him alone… only Him… Him alone.

I desire solitude… emptiness… and stillness, so as to plunge Myself into His pain and into His love!

Humbled by His favors and repentant for my sins, today my heart bursts…. Its love, and tenderness are overflowing, and I cannot stop loving this Jesus, wounded and agonizing because of the enormous weight of my crimes and ingratitude.

My soul is overflowing, my heart bursts, and in the madness of my love, today in my delirium and my sorrow, I propel myself to take You into my arms, Jesus, Jesus… to take Your injured Head into my hands, and having it *so very near* right in front of me, to talk to You with a greater love… to prick my forehead with the thorns of Your crown, and gather those threads of blood that extract love *more than pain*, from Your temples.

Thus… thus I want to contemplate my work! … and with my kisses… and with my caresses… and with my breath… and with my tears, cleanse and wash those eyes in whose pupils I see a portrait of myself… those lips that know only how to smile at me from the depth of pain… those slapped cheeks… the lily white forehead, pierced because of my countless vanities!

O Jesus, Word of my life! ... Your divine face, my Lord, slapped and spat upon by the world? ... O no, never! When that happened, I was not alive! But now, here is my face, O my Treasure! And a thousand faces if I could have them!

For me, Jesus, Jesus, my beloved Jesus! ... For me the spittle... the blows... the bruises... the blood... and the thorns! But for You? O my Heaven, my Treasure, my Passion! For You... light, tenderness, kisses, sighs, caresses, the dawn, the breeze! For You, love, tenderness! For You... a thousand heavens!

For me, O yes, yes, my charming Jesus, for me — scorn, humiliation, disdain, martyrdom — should it not be that way?

I do not deserve those pearls, and much less being a victim, and comforting You; but today is a day of graces, and You will give me the grace of pain... the grace of exchanging places... of transforming myself in You to bear the burden, because You, as You are now glorified, can no longer suffer, but living and throbbing in my heart, with Your help, I can go through Calvary again for Your glory and for Your love.

Let them trample over me, Jesus, let them plunge me into the mud; let them hate me and abhor me and dump me into a pigsty, so that they do not touch You... so that they do not hurt You... so that You may have a throne and so that they may love You, so that they may love You, my Lord, so that every heart may love You.

And why is it that they do not love You dearly, my Jesus?

Let me wipe Your forehead... let me press it against my heart... O what cruel and pricking thorns! Will You give them all to me, *all of them*, so that they may pierce my body and my heart?

Let me kiss You a thousand, thousand times with the warmth of my tenderness... I know that I can soil You with the mud of my contact, my Jesus, but what can I do? Lord, Lord! Tell me, what can I do with so much love?

You see, Jesus, my kisses are worth nothing — but not one of them is for anybody else. You know it... they are only Yours... only for You.... Your feet and Your side and Your neck and Your eyes are my delight. O if only, with all my tenderness in every one of those loving kisses, I could imprint, empty, and condense my soul! But my kisses, and even my heart, are so cold! Poverty, misery, and waste beyond compare!

And even so, my Life, my love is so great that You must put up with my caresses... because You are all mine!

But, this Jesus, mine? What can I do with You, Heart of my soul? O my Lord! Let me press

You against my heart, and do not feel disgusted with me because I disgust myself. What would I not give to be pure and clean so that I could be pleasing to You?

I am a sinner... base; but nonetheless, I die from joy belonging to You.

"All of Jesus!" I say, enamored. He is all mine! and I am all His! O what a delirium of love! He, humiliated and bloodied, and I, not humiliated and bloodied? Impossible! I must make myself like Him.

O Jesus, Jesus, my Jesus of all my soul! If I have You here... if nobody sees us... if only the angels hear us... if I love You so much... if I tremble with sorrow on contemplating You... if I fall into ecstasy counting Your sorrows... if the hours fly by... if I wish to suffer... if You are mine, all and forever mine!

But, what am I doing, my Jesus?

O my Lord and my God! O beloved Jesus of my life! Go back to Your Cross and forgive my audacity. But as You are my Heaven, my Master, my Love and my All, I will propel my-self to seize You, my Life! to bring You down from that Cross so that with my tears You would be cleansed from my sins and from the sins of others.

But, O my Lord! Why do You not speak to me, my Treasure? It goes without saying that You did not speak to Herod, but with me, who loves You so, so much that I eat You, that I drink You, that I inhale You and exhale You, and I am so happy just trying to decipher You... no, do not do this to me, no, for I am dying to hear You and to accomplish Your desires.

What do You desire, my Jesus, what do You desire?

"That you love Me," (You answer me)... "that you sacrifice yourself, renounce and die to yourself, always choosing whatever is more painful... that you soothe My face with your caresses and with your love... that you hide Me, finally, My child, that you hide Me, because I wish to hide Myself in order to rest."

I would like to open my heart, Lord, to make a crevice in it, a very hidden wound where no one could find You.

But, what are You asking from me with that look, my Treasure, what do You desire, what would I not give You even if it were necessary for me to rip my soul and tear my heart into shreds?

Do you wish me to be transformed into a cross? Well I will be the cross in life and in death, provided that You can rest upon it, provided that I can see You known, loved, and never offended! ... My heart breaks into pieces with pain upon seeing You despised... upon knowing that people do not think about You, and knowing that there are souls who hate You!

O Heart of my Beloved! The tepidity of Your own people… the sins of the world and Your delicate complaints, make my life bitter, and I suffer because You suffer.

But do not cry, my Jesus, no! Do not let those pupils which reflect heaven be dimmed by tears!

I am worth nothing; but as long as I live I shall be priest and victim in union with You. I love You — and very intensely — in the midst of Your suffering, thus torn apart and drained of blood, naked, desolate and forsaken!

I feel as if I will die when I contemplate You, but thus You attract me more, Lord: torn, crucified, in the most humiliating pain, in most loving scorn and oblivion.

And do You know why, my Jesus? Because You are the divine Model of suffering… because I want to accompany You where few will follow You… because I desire to resemble my Beloved.

My soul aspires to a life of martyrdom for love of You… and only that life of sacrifice and union on Calvary satisfies my spirit.

My Jesus, I no longer desire worldly things, human affection or comforts; my delight from now on will be abandonment and desolation which purify and transform even when they may be costly.

You want me to hide You in the hollow of

my heart, and I will not move from this spot unless You forever hide me in the place which the lance opened in Your side.

Jesus, Jesus, my crucified Jesus! Listen to me, and form out of all my being a living image of Him Who is my LOVE. O Jesus, grant that, even as a remote imitation of Mary, Your poor child may be a living cross, a voluntary martyr, a victim at the side of Mary of Sorrows. Amen.

Jesus, Savior of Mankind, Save Us!